GEOCACHING
HIKE AND SEEK WITH YOUR GPS

GEOCACHING
HIKE AND SEEK WITH YOUR GPS

Erik Sherman

Apress®

Geocaching: Hike and Seek with Your GPS

Copyright © 2004 by Erik Sherman

Technical Reviewer: Kelly Markwell

Editorial Board: Steve Anglin, Dan Appleman, Gary Cornell, James Cox,
Tony Davis, John Franklin, Chris Mills, Steve Rycroft, Dominic Shakeshaft, Julian Skinner,
Jim Sumser, Karen Watterson, Gavin Wray, John Zukowski

Project Manager: Sofia Marchant

Copy Manager: Nicole LeClerc

Copy Editor: Scott Carter

Production Manager: Kari Brooks

Production Editor: Ellie Fountain

Proofreader: Elizabeth Berry

Compositor: Gina Rexrode, Point n' Click Publishing, LLC

Indexer: Kevin Broccoli

Artist: Kinetic Publishing Services, LLC

Cover Designer: Kurt Krames

Manufacturing Manager: Tom Debolski

Library of Congress Cataloging-in-Publication Data

Sherman, Erik B.

Geocaching : hike and seek with your GPS / Erik Sherman.
p. cm. -- (Technology in action series)
Includes bibliographical references and index.
ISBN-13: 978-1-59059-122-2 (soft cover : alk. paper)
ISBN-10: 1-59059-122-4 (soft cover : alk. paper)
1. Geocaching (Game) 2. Global Positioning System. I. Title. II. Series.

GV1202.G46S54 2004
623.89--dc22

2004004803

Printed and bound in the United States of America (POD)

Trademarked names may appear in this book. Rather than use a trademark symbol with every occurrence of a trademarked name, we use the names only in an editorial fashion and to the benefit of the trademark owner, with no intention of infringement of the trademark.

Distributed to the book trade in the United States by Springer-Verlag New York, Inc., 233 Spring Street, Sixth Floor New York, NY 10013 and outside the United States by Springer-Verlag GmbH & Co. KG, Tiergartenstr. 17, 69112 Heidelberg, Germany.

In the United States: phone 1-800-SPRINGER, e-mail orders@springer-ny.com, or visit http://www.springer-ny.com. Outside the United States: fax +49 6221 345229, e-mail orders@springer.de, or visit http://www.springer.de.

For information on translations, please contact Apress directly at 2560 Ninth Street, Suite 219, Berkeley, CA 94710. Phone 510-549-5930, fax 510-549-5939, e-mail info@apress.com, or visit http://www.apress.com.

The information in this book is distributed on an "as is" basis, without warranty. Although every precaution has been taken in the preparation of this work, neither the author(s) nor Apress shall have any liability to any person or entity with respect to any loss or damage caused or alleged to be caused directly or indirectly by the information contained in this work.

This book is dedicated to all the people who realized that a technology developed for the military can be used peacefully when you are hiking a million miles from your nearest worldly care. Special thanks go to Lisa, Allie, and Matt for putting up with another engulfing project. Who needs a GPSr to find your way home when you have a family?

Contents at a Glance

Contents

About the Author

Erik Sherman knows what it's like to get lost on foot, in the woods, in a car, and even under water, so when he learned about GPS, he was hooked. He is a freelance writer and photographer, and his work has appeared in such publications as the *New York Times Magazine*, *Newsweek*, *US News & World Report*, *USA Weekend*, *Financial Times*, *Continental*, *Chief Executive*, *Columbia Journalism Review*, and *Red Herring*. He is the author of two books on home networking and one on Pocket PCs.

About the Technical Reviewer

 **Kelly Markwell** is a 37-year-old Technical Support Technician in the Chicago, Illinois suburbs (roughly N 41° 38', W 088° 14'). He has been geocaching since March of 2001 with his wife and two sons. He has a degree in music education and taught in public schools for several years before taking a job in the computer industry. Geocaching drew his attention as a meld of two of his favorite hobbies: hiking and technology. Most of the knowledge he has gained regarding geocaching and land navigation comes from his being an avid participant of the Groundspeak forums on geocaching, where he learns from the wealth of knowledge of others. He is an active participant in both geocaching and geodashing.

Acknowledgments

I'd like to acknowledge many people and organizations that made this book possible. Thanks to Kelly Markwell for helping to keep the subject on course and Scott Carter to similarly keep my grammar oriented. Ellie Fountain has been a great help with the graphics, and Sofia Marchant has been humane about cracking the whip to keep all of us doing what we should. John Zukowski, the original acquisitions editor, and the editorial board were gracious in giving me a chance to write this book when one New York publishing house after another wrinkled their brows and passed.

Thanks to Steve Donelan, Elizabeth Keifer, and Karen Berger, all outdoors experts who spared various amounts of time to answer my questions about natural surroundings obscurities. I also want to thank the following companies: Brunton, Outdoor Research, Vasque, LEKI USA, Gregory Mountain Products, Black Diamond, Garmin, Magellan, and HP. Last but not least, I want to thank the geocaching community—people genuine in their interest and generous with their time, if on occasion contentious in their presentations.

Preface

It isn't often that you witness the birth of a new sport or game. I'm not referring to some variation on a theme, like snowboarding on your hands, or to one of the prepackaged amusements that erupt like a volcano of marketing froth during the holiday seasons, but a real game—one that catches the imagination and quickly develops a cadre of devoted followers without dollar one spent on promotion.

That is how I think of geocaching, enabled by cutting-edge technology and started on one man's whim. From its beginning as an insider's activity involving dozens of people who participated in an electronic newsgroup about GPS technology, geocaching has sprung forth to intrigue and interest people in so many countries that it would seem easier to name those who haven't yet been touched by it.

Almost anyone can find some appeal in geocaching: for the gadget hound, electronics; for puzzle fans, mental challenges; for outdoor enthusiasts, hiking, boating, climbing, and diving; and for parents, a chance to get kids away from video screens and have them burn off some energy. People of all ages play— I've heard of toddlers out with their parents and retired couples enjoying a mutual interest.

Winter, summer, sun, rain, day, night—almost any time and place can be right for geocaching. Hidden containers are waiting to be found in Antarctica and, probably, just around the corner from you. So, certainly, read about geocaching, but then get on your feet, out the door, and start looking: the game is on.

Starting Off

"The beginning is the most important part of the work."—Plato

As the numbers drop, I move faster. Dried twigs snap, leaves rustle. I'm on the hunt this late autumn morn. The display on my GPS receiver shows 517 . . . 453 . . . 326. Although I've been hiking for several miles, my body urges me to run, but I must resist, keeping my senses alert to avoid missing the quarry. The count drops, drops—well under 200 feet—then suddenly starts to climb. I freeze and look behind me. I see a small opening in the trees and brush. Entering, I follow a minor trail into a clearing, once the foundation of a cabin with a spectacular lake view. Just inside the ring of stone, two large pieces of birch bark nestled below one of the rocks look suspicious. I move them and find it: a geocache. A plastic container placed in a hollow contains knick-knacks. Opening it, I place a plastic pen and take a pin—my trophy. The container goes back into its corner and the bark into place.

This is the new activity of geocaching: part treasure hunt, part outdoor exploration. It owes its birth in 2000 to human ingenuity, the Internet, and Global Positioning System (GPS) technology. The concept is simple. One person puts together a collection of things—toys, mementos, trinkets—and places them in a container, called the *cache*, takes a reading of its position with a GPS device, then posts the location numbers on a Web site. Someone else looks up the location, finds the cache, takes one item from the collection, and replaces it with another.

It sounds easy; you can choose to take a short walk down a well-manicured trail in a park to a cache that you discover after a few minutes of looking. Or you can select a hunt that involves hiking into mountains or remote wilderness and searching for an hour—or far longer—to find the container. You can find caches tucked away in urban nooks and crannies, or on cliff faces that require the seeker to rappel down to reach the hiding place. Geocaching can be as domestic as the wooded area just a five-minute walk from your home, or as exotic as scuba diving 100 feet down off the coast of Bimini to find the final clue to a cache. You can hunt for dime-store knickknacks and toys from fast-food restaurants, or participate in contests for thousands of dollars, or just find caches for the bragging rights. Go for solo jaunts, or take along others. Enjoy the health benefits of physical activity, the pleasure of play, the aesthetic delight in the natural world, and the challenge of a puzzle, all at the same time.

The experience is as varied as the possibilities, and can lead to moments stolen out of time. A few miles from where I live, on a street I sometimes take as a shortcut, a single quiet road heads off to the side. Over the years, I had never wondered what lay down there. In fact, its existence barely registered with me. Early in my geocaching experience, one nearby cache had me circling a large undeveloped area. Finally sitting down with an online map, I noticed this road and how it seemed to extend toward the cache location. Taking that turn for the first time, I found myself pulling into a dead end where a plaque for a memorial forest stood. It was overcast, a little drizzly, and wet from previous rain. I marched in, following the readings on my GPS unit, kept to a trail, past an insignificant offshoot, and ever closer to the final spot. It seemed to be off the trail on the border of a marsh. Slowly I dodged and weaved past bramble, which grows faster than rumors where I live. Five feet, ten feet, twenty: progress was slow, and I had yet to learn the lesson that when a shortcut seems advisable, the searcher is usually delusional. A foot in the damp muck finally convinced me, and I looked around, then noticed that just beyond bramble thick enough to audition for a production of *Sleeping Beauty* there seemed to be another trail: that blasted offshoot that I had ignored.

Being no prince, and seeing no thorn magically turn away, I moved back, regained the main trail, and then took that branch. I wove past walls of grass and bush until the path moved onto a land spit gesturing out into the marsh. In the distance was a major road I had taken thousands of times. I had seen this marsh from the other side, without realizing that it was possible to move this easily into it. The GPS readings suggested that the hiding place was a little depression to the left, with the cache probably behind a tree. Then I heard a loud fluttering; off to the right were two wild ducks beating their wings, lifting themselves off from the wetlands and taking to the air. Then there was a deep rasping, and a large dark bird with a neck like a swan's glided in for a rest. It was a great blue heron, a bird I have never seen live. Sure, I found the cache hidden behind a small clump of trees, but the experience was the real magic.

Why Do It?

Sentimental thoughts of drifting magic pixie dust aside, geocaching is a wonderful way to spend time apart from the demands of work and life. There are many reasons to take up the activity.

Health

Although you can pursue geocaching in different ways, I haven't heard of caches hidden at drive-up windows. By its nature, geocaching requires that you be out and on your feet and moving around. If you become even moderately involved, you could easily find yourself walking miles each week that you would never have done had it been planned "exercise." Depending on your athletic prowess and the vigor with which you pursue the quarry, you can leave yourself in a heavy sweat and burn hundreds of calories in a single hunt. And if you are the type who hates exercise for its own sake, hunting some caches can get you moving about, even against your better judgment.

Family Togetherness

A good number of geocachers involve their families, from youngest to oldest. On the very first search I undertook, I brought my wife, our two children, plus four siblings who were staying with us that weekend. Even though it was cold and damp, the kids absolutely loved the whole process. We gave each a little something to trade and went to some nearby trails to find a cache hidden a good half mile in. The boy who actually spotted the container in a dead tree trunk got first choice of the loot, and the others lined up to see what they might get. The parents of the visiting horde said that their children were talking about the experience for a week after.

Education

Hand in glove with family is education. Despite even the most recalcitrant nine-year-old's worst of intentions, it is impossible to participate in geocaching without learning something. To navigate, you can use a compass in addition to the GPS unit, and that means math. Maps mean geography. Global positioning is science. Discovering a cache requires patience and logic. Many caches are in sites with historic significance. Working with others requires teamwork. And hiking through forests, mountains, and wildlife preserves provides opportunities to learn about natural science and ecology. Even an adult might learn something.

Natural Beauty

It is painfully easy to forget to smell the roses—or see the pine trees or hear a noisy brook—when dealing with daily life. Cell phones, television, the Internet, video games, and the remaining roster of consumer electronics can keep your head spinning. But geocaching is an activity that, ironically, uses technology to direct you toward the natural world. From the austere majesty of mountains and deserts to the contemplative consideration of trees in a park, you can find a sense of psychic renewal.

Challenge

The Rolling Stones said "you can't always get what you want," but that is actually much of the fun in life. If everything were easy, nothing would matter. In geocaching, you can choose whatever level of challenge you'd like on a given day. Caches are listed with rankings for terrain and difficulty. Choose a cache that should be easy to find but that requires a good, long hike. Chase after one that could have you scratching your head for an hour when you arrive at the final coordinates. Undertake cache hunts that require kayaking, or rock climbing, or scuba diving, or mountaineering, or puzzle solving.

Discovery

You might be amazed at the things you pass in your everyday life. There are so many enclaves of nature, so much history, so much that is just plain curious. Geocaching will take your hand and lead you to one spot after another, all hidden in the open, that you'd never otherwise have known existed. Almost every time I go, I find another delightful surprise.

Fun

It's a good time. Exercise your wanderlust, meet others for geocaching events, enjoy choosing your trophy from the cache, and have a good excuse for a beer at the end of the day.

Who Geocaches?

Geocaching is for everyone. All right, maybe not everyone, but for a surprising variety. One is a septuagenarian grandmother. Another, when she isn't attending high school, goes geocaching with her friends. A semiretired couple living a few miles from me geocaches. Geocachers are all over the world: in England and New England and New Guinea, in Finland and Florida. They live across the continent and across the street. Programmers are involved, and so are secretaries and celebrities.

Whether you think of geocaching as a sport with strenuous hikes through mountains and technical rock climbing, or as a game about finding tiny treasures, it has its appeal—so much so that the activity has grown from a few dozen enthusiasts at its onset to hundreds of thousands just two years later. And, as more companies realize just how much people enjoy geocaching, its growth may really take off.

One reason for the expanding interest is the small price required to begin participating. The only required equipment is a handheld GPS receiver, and models start at under $100. The government covered the biggest expense through tax money—we all chipped in about $40 each, all 200-odd million of us. What do you get for the money? Something very expnsive.

GPS History

Geocaching is possible only because the U.S. Department of Defense developed the Global Positioning System as a navigation aid for the armed forces at a cost of about $12 billion since the 1970s, and that cost is likely to double over the next decade or two.

The reason for the big numbers is the equipment necessary to make GPS work: dozens of satellites in continuous orbit around the globe. Special receivers with access to the open sky detect the signals and, using some sophisticated and clever mathematics and electronics theory, determine the operator's position, direction, and speed anywhere on earth.

At first, the GPS technology was a military secret. A civilian version was available, but it was severely restricted though a program called Selective Availability (SA). Users without proper security clearance could find positions only within roughly 300 feet (100 meters) of their actual locations. However, in May 2000 President Clinton signed an executive order directing the military to stop scrambling GPS signals.

It was suddenly possible for anyone to buy a GPS receiver and get the full benefit of the system. Instead of finding position within the length of an American football field, users could determine a location to within a tenth of that distance, or better. No small coincidence that people had developed the idea of geocaching within a couple of weeks of the change.

History of Geocaching

The term has been used only since 2000, and the game or sport itself is barely older. Originally called GPS Stash Hunt, it was the brainchild of David J. Ulmer, who created the first cache—containing a can of beans, a compass, and a videotape—in Oregon. Interest in the new activity quickly grew, but Ulmer officially dropped out of the game roughly a month after its creation out of concern for potential environmental damage of too many feet tromping over too many unspoiled parts of the planet, so he explains. (Later chapters discuss in depth how proper geocaching can not only prevent damage, but also can result in even cleaner areas and minimize unnecessary wandering about.)

The split between Ulmer and the rest of the players resulted in a fair degree of unpleasantness on both sides that turned into arguments and even name-calling on Internet discussion boards. In fact, the brief description of the game's history on Geocaching.com, the largest Internet site serving as the clearinghouse for announcing and following action at caches, fails to mention Ulmer by name. One name that does appear is Mike Teague, who built the first Web site for the game and found that first cache.

While he was still involved, Ulmer had second thoughts about the name of the game. Although GPS seemed a natural, stash had many negative connotations with drugs and illegal activities, and most everyone involved looked forward to the game becoming popular with the general public. "Doesn't seem to fit in today's spandex, natural, ecotourist world we now live in," he wrote at the time. A number of people began making suggestions, some of which, like *geosatplaneteering*, were unwieldy and would only have caused nightmares for unsuspecting marketers. Ulmer came close with the term *geostashing*, with the final variation suggested by another player, Matt Stum, who wanted to substitute the word *cache* for *stash*. According to him, *cache* had been a name for any collection of food and supplies left by northern explorers. People who traveled a given trail would know about the caches, which were community property. If people needed something, they'd take it, and similarly leave their surplus. In addition, cache was a type of computer memory. The dual reference, historic and modern, got the popular nod after an online poll, and the game *geocaching* was born.

Predecessors

Geocaching is both a noun and verb that describes the game and the action of playing it. But the concept of hiding things and seeking them is older than the onset of the twenty-first century. According to Geocaching.com, since the 1980s a group of Finns in Helsinki have played a variation on orienteering in which they hunt locations with compass and map. The members introduced GPS systems in the 1990s to check accuracy, so they could be the original geocachers.

Even at that, games requiring searching are ancient. The children's game of hide-and-seek can be traced back more than 4,000 years. A number of magician's basic entertainments, such as tricks where cards go missing only to reappear later, or balls seeming to hop from one overturned cup to another, are based on this same principle. The two activities that seem most like parents, though, are the letterboxing game and orienteering.

In 1854, James Perrot was a guide in Dartmoor, a region of moors and wooded valleys that is now a national park in southwest England. In one area called Cranmere Pool, a relatively inaccessible point in the high moors, Perrot left copies of his Victorian calling card in a glass bottle for people to find, proving that they had reached the point. Each visitor would also leave a self-addressed postcard. The next visitor would retrieve the card and send it upon returning home. The practice expanded slowly over the next few decades to five letterboxes.

This developed into a pastime using rubber stamps. A participant has a personal stamp and logbook. Each letterbox also has its own stamp and book. People who find a letterbox use their stamp on the log at the box and then mark their own log with the box's stamp. Because some people still place postcards in the letterboxes, participants do drop the cards in the mail. To find a box, those playing the game share with each other clues that include a reference to a map grid, compass bearings from a landmark, and a specified number of paces. Books and Internet sites list many of these letterbox clues. Millions of people enjoy letterboxing; there are tens of thousands of registered letterboxes, and many more that are not.

Orienteering, the other parent activity, officially started in 1897. Using compass and map, participants race over a course that can be wilderness forest, park, or desert. Each person must proceed along a series of designated points, punching cards at each location in turn. Whoever has the fastest time wins, but many people, from young children to nonagenarians, play for recreation, and single orienteering meets have been known to attract tens of thousands. Not only is orienteering played on foot, but also on mountain bikes and cross-country skis.

Exploding Popularity

Still, the child might outreach the parent, and geocaching could become more popular than either predecessor over time. It has been one of those examples of viral marketing, a modern term for word-of-mouth as happens only on the Internet. At last count (this number jumps faster than I can look it up), more than 88,000 active caches in 188 countries were listed on Geocaching.com, only one of several similar sites. Companies are beginning to notice the geocaching market, and at least one firm is developing corporate team-building events based on geocaching. Welcome to a booming trend.

Although it is easy to become involved, you do need to learn some skills: use of GPS devices, navigation with compass and map, hiking preparation, integrating other technology, and geocaching etiquette, among others. You will learn these skills and more in this book. The best place to start is at the heart of the game.

Cache On

"Our treasure lies in the beehive of our knowledge."
—Friedrich Nietzsche

In its simplest form, geocaching is an easy concept to grasp. *Hiders*—
geocachers who enjoy setting up caches for others to find—pick collections
of items and put them into containers, which they then hide, somewhere,
say out in a public park or state forest, after ensuring with the appropriate
agencies that this activity will be condoned. Other people, *seekers*, try to find the
containers, generally taking items from containers, replacing them with others,
and going on their ways. How do people know where they've hidden containers,
or where to find them? Why, by using their trusty GPS receivers, of course—at
least usually.

Simple, no? Well, no, there's a little more to it than that. The process of
finding a cache is generally a series of steps:

1. Go to a geocaching Web site and choose a cache you want to find.

2. Enter the coordinates in your GPS receiver.

3. Print the description and, if you want, any clues that may help in case
   things are tougher than you expected.

4. Go find the cache and make a note in its log book.

5. Enter your results on the cache Web page.

Similarly, hiding a cache also requires a series of steps:

1. Scout a location removed from other caches and find a good hiding
   spot there.

2. Get any permission necessary.

3. Pull together an appropriate container and goodies, including a log book, to fill it.

4. Hide the cache in its new home and obtain coordinates as accurate as possible.

5. Post the cache on one of the geocaching Web sites.

6. Follow up on any e-mail comments or questions from people trying to find the cache.

7. Periodically check the condition of the cache and its environment.

As you might suspect, there are potential slipping points all along the way, which Chapters 6 and 7 cover. But you might have noticed mention of geocaching sites and Web pages. Most people involved with the hobby find a GPS receiver vital, but the one virtually indispensable bit of technology for geocaching is actually the Web. The game is played on a number of sites, and you need to know about them.

Caching Playgrounds

Paper and word of mouth are too slow for the pace of geocaching (although they do have a place, as we will discuss later). New cache locations have exploded in number since the onset of the pastime; tens of thousands are now available around the world. To keep up, hiders and seekers communicate on the Web.

Think of the Internet as a meeting ground, or maybe a virtual playground when you aren't out in the woods. Although I describe a number of useful Web sites in later chapters, four sites will take most of your attention:

- Geocaching.com

- Navicache.com

- Buxley's Geocaching Waypoint

- Opencaching.com

These are the major outlets for cache listings and information, and you need to become acquainted with each.

Geocaching.com

This is the successor of the original geocaching site and is still the largest. Figure 2-1 shows the home page.

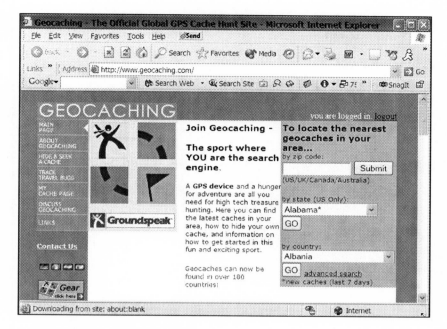

Figure 2-1 Geocaching.com home page

On the left is a menu. You can choose the following:

- About Geocaching: This gives a brief and incomplete history of geocaching.

- Hide & Seek A Cache: Here is where you click to either submit a cache for others to find, or to choose a cache you want to hunt.

- Track Travel Bugs: Travel bugs are objects that people find in one cache and move to another. You can follow their journeys here. (And you can follow the topic in Chapter 8.)

- My Cache Page: If you have an account (free at the basic level and worth getting) you can check a listing of caches in your area, see your lists of found caches, and any caches you have created.

- Discuss Geocaching: If you have questions or just want to chat, you can go to message boards, again free, and correspond with others active in the sport.

- Links: You can find links to useful software and other sites of interest to the geocacher.

Before going through the menu, though, scroll down the home page until you see the heading *Create an Account*. Click on the *Create an account now* link and fill out the fields. This will give you access to most of the forum, including the important ability to log your caching finds and to list the caches you hide. After all, bragging rights go a short distance if you don't keep score.

To get a start on searching, go to the upper-right corner of the home page, enter your zip code, and click the *Submit* button. That will bring you to a page similar to that in Figure 2-2.

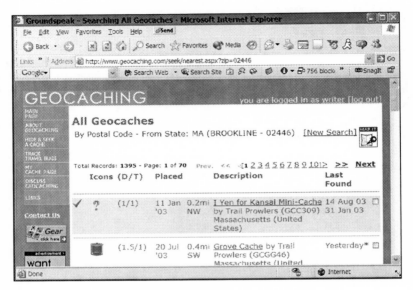

Figure 2-2 Example of a cache search page

The caches appear with such information as the date they first appeared on the site, the user name of the person who placed the cache, and the distance from your zip code. (The distance is calculated from the post office serving that area.) A checkmark shows that you have already completed the cache. An icon indicates the type of cache.

Two important numbers are the difficulty and terrain ratings (the D/T column). Both use a 1-to-5 scale, with 1 being easy and 5 being difficult. Some factors contributing to the difficulty rating include the length of the hike to the cache, the difficulty of finding the cache, or whether there are difficult puzzles to solve before you can find the cache. Terrain includes the amount of slope, the footing, nature of the trail, whether an overnight stay is necessary, and the need for specialized training or equipment in such areas as scuba diving or technical rock climbing. A 1/1 cache is one you could take kids to on a whim, whereas a 5/5 might have you backpacking or searching a cliff face a hundred feet (30-odd meters) in the air.

The home page also has a link to a *Benchmark Hunting* section, an activity in which you search for survey markers that are physical references for location and height. (More on benchmarking in Chapter 8.)

One thing to remember about this site is that it's a business, as opposed to some of the other sites, which seem more like quasi-hobbies run by enthusiasts. Nothing wrong with that, but it does mean that there is more organizational control over what goes onto the site, including what will and won't be allowed for caches, as well as what may be posted in the discussion forums. As with any degree of effectiveness, there is good and bad. On the positive side, the staff is careful about caches that appear in areas they shouldn't (like national parks, where they are not allowed) or that are too close to other caches. The negatives can include a perceived censorship, like people finding that their posts mentioning competing geocaching sites are deleted. Others are concerned that the management is trying to own geocaching.

My own complaint is that the pages are generally too crowded, and sometimes important links—such as benchmarking or signing up for an account—are buried in the text and not called out in the navigation areas.

> **NOTE** Around the time we were making final edits on the book, I heard that Geocaching.com was preparing to make some changes in the look of its site. Unfortunately, prototypes won't be available until this book is actually in print, so you may have to make some mental adjustments.

On the balance, I like the site and the people who run it have my respect. I also think that geocaching is quickly becoming too big for any one group to control, and that is why some competition is good.

Navicache.com

Our second caching stop is Navicache.com. As is true with Geocaching.com and Buxley's Geocaching Waypoint, there is a navigation menu, though at the top of the screen. And like Geocaching.com, the home page also has a search area, as Figure 2-3 shows.

A difference, though, is that you can search by city and state as well as by zip code in the United States, or by latitude and longitude elsewhere in the world (see Chapter 4) to look for caches. The number of caches and the amount of activity is small compared to Geocaching.com. The two sites have slightly different criteria for approving caches, so you might find that one allows something that the other doesn't.

One of the menu choices leads to the next virtual stop, Buxley's Geocaching Waypoint.

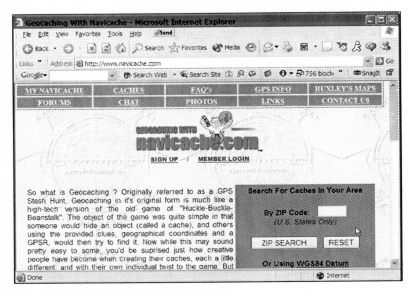

Figure 2-3 Navicache.com home page

Buxley's Geocaching Waypoint

This site, `http://www.brillig.com/geocaching/`, is unusual because it does not host cache Web pages. (See Figure 2-4.)

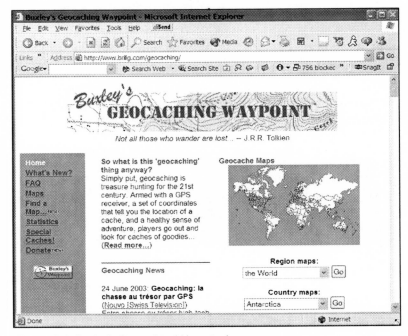

Figure 2-4 Buxley's Geocaching Waypoint home page

Instead, Buxley's is a mapping site. It has searchable maps that show locations of different caches, giving you a more graphic approach to searching. Click on the map and the page switches to a bigger search map, as you can see in Figure 2-5.

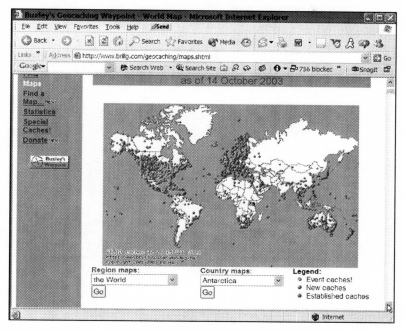

Figure 2-5 Search map on Buxley's Geocaching Waypoint

You can click to select a particular region, like the United States, and have it appear in more detail, as Figure 2-6 shows.

Notice all the bubbles that have appeared on these maps. Each represents a single cache. Blue bubbles are new caches, and green ones are event caches in which people are invited to meet on a particular day and time. The number of bubbles may be gratifying for the person who enjoys the game, but it's visually overwhelming if you are trying to choose a target, so select a smaller area, like the state of Massachusetts, as in Figure 2-7.

You can click again in this case and zoom in for more detailed views, though not all regions have enough cache density to warrant the closer view. When possible, as Figure 2-8 shows, you can pan the map in different directions by clicking the directional arrows corresponding to compass directions on the map's border.

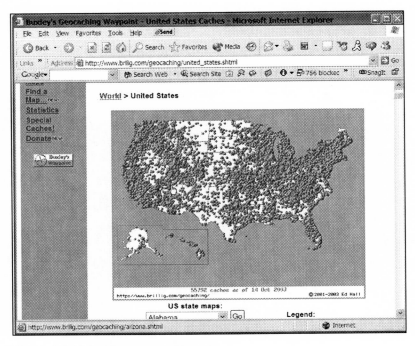

Figure 2-6 United States geocaching map

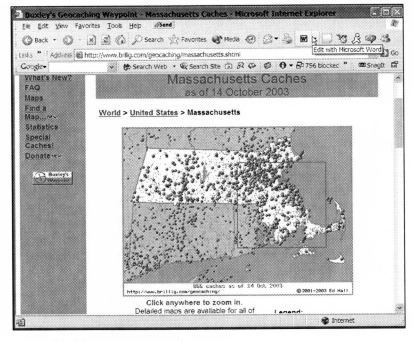

Figure 2-7 Massachusetts geocaching map

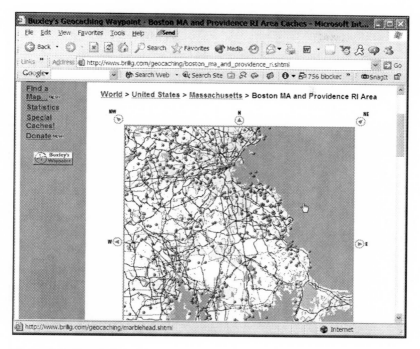

Figure 2-8 Detailed map

In this case, you can click for yet another closer view. Theoretically, Buxley's site regularly updates and adds all new caches from the other sites. Practically, you can't count on when that update will take place. After hiding a cache, I found that it did not appear on the site, at least for a while. Potential for human or computer error aside, it's a good resource, especially if you want to pick a location with a high density of caches for a hunting spree.

Should you want to skip a few of the map clicks, choose a region or country map from the boxes on the home page.

Another interesting spot is the *Statistics* menu choice at the left of the home page. Not only does the site calculate the number of caches you can find in any country, but it provides links to other sites that can tell you who is who when it comes to finding caches.

Opencaching.com

Both Geocaching.com and Navicache.com have online forums where people can discuss the activity and other related concerns. However, some people have voiced concern about geocaching effectively being the property of the companies that run those two sites. Opencaching.com is an attempt to create a nonproprietary electronic community for cachers. Is it necessary? I don't know, but its appearance is no clear detriment; stop by the site and make your own decision.

Caches

So far, you might have the sense that all caches, at heart, are the same, with only the details changing. That actually isn't true. There are many types of caches and related objects:

- Traditional
- Micros
- Multis
- Offset
- Puzzle
- Secret
- Virtual
- Moving
- Hitchhikers and Travel Bugs
- Benchmarks

Each type offers different challenges, advantages, and disadvantages. Let's take a look at them in a little more detail.

Traditional

These are classic caches, like the first one ever hidden. Someone takes a container, whether the plastic snap-lid type or a metal ammunition can, and puts items into it. (See Figure 2-9.)

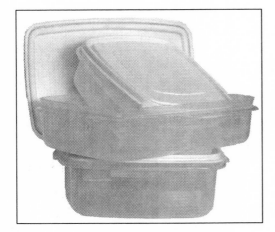

Figure 2-9 Some typical cache containers

The containers have the virtue of being largely watertight—an advantage when things stay out in the wild, whether woods or urban—and, if of good quality, not prone to breaking. In these days of paranoia, plastic has gained popularity because carrying a food container doesn't make you look as suspicious as an ammo can might. Items in the container generally include a collection of knick-knacks, toys, or items of potential interest, as well as a log book along with a pen or pencil so people can record their find. You can also find other items of interest:

- Souvenir items

- A camera

- Site-specific information

- Hitchhikers

A souvenir item is a commemorative to remind you of a particular cache. It can be a cachecard, which is a business card bearing the name of the cache and some other information, such as the name of the cache owner, coordinates of the cache, and a photograph of the spot. You can collect them or drop them off at other caches to spread the word about one you've visited. Some people invest in geocoins, like those shown in Figure 2-10.

Figure 2-10 Examples of geocoins

Geocoins are usually metal and embossed with a logo and a name, usually the name of a regional geocaching group or the cache's owners. If you want to make your own out of polymer clay, you can follow the directions of cacher MountainMudbug at `http://www.geocities.com/graphixoutpost/geocoins.html`.

The camera will be the disposable type, with a flash. This allows cache finders to take pictures of themselves or their group. The cache owner will occasionally pick up the camera when it would be running short of film, have it developed, then scan the pictures and post them on a Web page so people can see themselves.

Site-specific information, in the form of printed sheets that people can take, is rarer, but always fun. You can learn about the historical significance of a particular site, and there might be a sheet on an unusual type of tree or bird or animal. Any of this might add to your appreciation and enjoyment if you are inclined to such considerations. If not, feel free to ignore it.

Hitchhikers and their relatives, travel bugs, are items that move from cache to cache. I describe these later in the chapter.

Micros

Not all cache locations offer either enough space or cover from prying eyes to shelter a traditional container. There are also those cache owners who want to make a hunt at least challenging, if not difficult to the point of pain. For such situations, a cache can be a micro, like the ones in Figure 2-11.

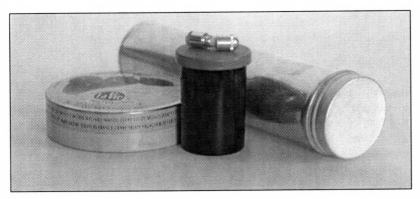

Figure 2-11 Micro cache containers

A favorite, and on the larger side of micro, is an empty 35mm film canister. A metal mints container, like those from Altoids, are also popular, although it takes some work to remove the mint odor; otherwise, you run the risk of attracting animals. Micro caches create two other difficulties: finding objects to put in the cache, and having a log book and pencil small enough to fit within.

Things get tougher when you have even smaller caches, because the lower limits of size are restricted only by the ingenuity of people bent on confounding their fellows. A cache in the greater Boston area is actually a coin superglued to a powerful magnet and left in an unlikely place. To get credit for the find, you must e-mail the country and date of the coin to the cache owner. Unfortunately, Geocaching.com has stopped approving these sorts of caches, but there is a solution. I've hidden a micro called Classical Cache with a small log for people to sign. However, to get credit, you must answer some questions listed in the container, e-mail the responses to me, and get approval to claim the find. The latter was an idea that I cheerfully stole from a number of other cachers.

Speaking of coins, another cacher hid a little object significantly smaller than a penny. The cache description suggests bringing a magnifying glass and a pair of tweezers to handle the object. No, the person wasn't kidding. You could spend a good long time finding this one, and on its side are the coordinates for another cache, because it is part of a multi-cache.

Multis

I've spoken with a number of cachers whose favorite type of cache is the multi, or multi-cache. In a multi, the published coordinates are for a single cache, usually a micro cache. Inside (or, as described previously, on the side) are the coordinates for another cache, which could house coordinates for yet another. As a variation, seekers may have to find multiple caches, not necessarily in any particular order, to obtain the various parts of the coordinates for the final stage.

After finding the first, you reset the waypoint to the new coordinates and find the next container. This can go on for as many stages as the owner and hunter have patience. They are greatly enjoyable because you are on the chase for a while, and you obtain a feeling of accomplishment at the end. The final stage is often a traditional cache, with lots of goodies for the persistent cacher.

Offset

In some cases, the published coordinates are not even for the actual cache. Instead, you are directed to a spot from which you must follow directions to the cache location. The directions might be a compass bearing or azimuth that you must follow for a certain number of steps (more on this in Chapter 4), or they may direct you to travel along a line created by a series of landmarks.

Sometimes, the offset cache is created for the hider to flex some creative muscle and for the seeker to invoke some patience and determination. At other times, an offset may be the only practical way of providing a usable location.

For example, a cache in my area is called Miller's Wood. The actual cache location is in a forest, heavy with hemlock and birch trees of a century's age. However, as you will learn in Chapter 3, those trees can play havoc with the reception of a GPS receiver, leaving you unable to follow an electronic course to the loot. The cache owners, a semiretired couple who go by the name GeoChevy50, realized the problem, and so gave some guidelines in terms of descriptions of certain trees. I went directly to `Google.com` on the Internet to look up the appropriate pictures, as my woodsman's skills are what you might expect from a child of suburbia.

Many geocachers might disagree that Miller's Wood is an offset cache, but to my mind, if you can't reliably get there by a GPS receiver and you need additional help to find the location, it's offset.

Puzzle

Multi-caches present an increased element of the challenge over the traditional. Offset caches introduce indirection. Puzzle caches take all this a step further. Instead of offering coordinates to the actual location, the seeker—that is, you—has to solve some puzzles, either intellectual or physical, to reach the cache.

An example is my own Fighting Silver Cache, listed on Geocaching.com, which also shares some of the attributes of an offset cache. In it, the coordinates are only to a parking lot. You bring a compass and follow some clues to shoot two bearings (yes, that is also in Chapter 4) to pinpoint the actual place to search. It's a relatively simple one—mild compared to some that are far more complicated.

For example, another cache in my state is the Raiders of the Lost Geocache. It's worth checking the site on Geocaching.com, even if you aren't close enough to pursue it. The coordinates are real enough, but you must go to an additional Web page for the information you will need, because this is an offset puzzle cache. (See Figure 2-12.)

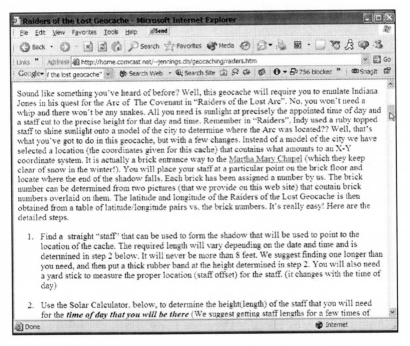

Figure 2-12 Web page for Raiders of the Lost Geocache

You must determine ahead at what day and time you will attempt this, after checking a weather site for a forecast. The weather is important because you need a good shadow produced by the sun. The Raiders site has a program into which you enter the day and time information. In return, you get a measurement. This is the height of the stick you must bring with you.

The coordinates bring you to an overhang with a brick floor. Diagrams on the site, combined with a table, give a long list of potential coordinates. By planting the stick in the proper place and observing the brick on which the top of the shadow falls, you find the corresponding coordinates, which will take you to the real cache location. (See Figure 2-13.)

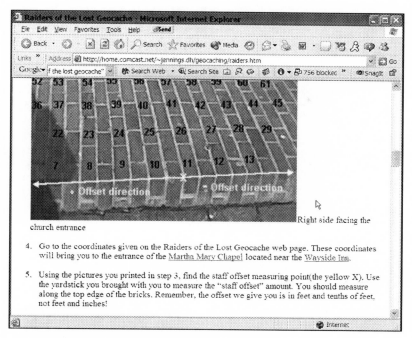

Figure 2-13 Diagram of how the Raiders cache works

Involved? Yes. Ingenious? Absolutely. Have I done it yet? Not at the time of writing, but it's on my short list. The instructions suggest bringing a tape measure and a saw so that if you are running late, you can trim the stick, if necessary, to the correct length. Instead, I'll probably rig a perpendicular flag that I can move to different heights. That should show where the top of the shadow of a stick that particular height would have fallen. However, I'll also bring a saw—just in case.

NOTE In British Columbia, Canada, a group called Team KFWB indulges in the most extravagant of cache hunts, with first-finder packages of loot that run into the thousands of dollars in value. Oh, but to find the cache, you need ingenuity, persistence, effort spread over days, access to four-wheel-drive vehicles, and the ability to follow specific instructions to assemble the coordinates of the cache location. Don't plan on getting rich, though. I spoke with someone who had worked as part of a group solving a couple of these, and between the number of searchers and the time needed, the monetary reward on an hourly basis would make entry-level burger-flipping look good.

Some puzzle caches require a strong bent for riddles and intellectual twists. For those, some preliminary research on the Internet, or in a library, can do wonders.

Secret

For some caches, research is unlikely to help at all. These are secret caches, whose coordinates do not appear on a page at one of the major caching sites. In some cases, there is a page, but only with general information and instructions.

There is a cacher in Rhode Island who keeps a Web page devoted to his activities. On it is a link to a "bonus" cache in the state. You cannot find the coordinates, or even the cache's existence, any other way. How did I find out about it? By reading a New England geocaching forum and running across a mention of the site, with a link. Word of mouth pays off, and makes it hard for a secret to remain *too* secret. I'd include a link for the page, but then it wouldn't be secret.

Virtual

Sometimes a cache can be out for everyone to see, but only those playing the game can claim credit of discovery. That is because not all caches are physical. In some places, like the U.S. National Parks, you are not allowed to leave items, even caches. In other spots, like many cities, too many people might wander by and see someone retrieve a cache, only to return to the site and steal the container, leaving everyone else out of luck. (Yes, people have plundered caches.)

In such settings, a virtual cache may be in order. With this type, you don't open a container, trade items, and sign a log. Instead, you collect proof that you can send to the cache owner. It might be information contained on a placard attached to a building's exterior wall, or it could be a digital photo you e-mail to the cache owner.

An example is the Masonic Home Virtual Cache in Wisconsin. If seeking this cache, you follow the directions and find a historic marker, then answer a question by using the information on it. The answer to the question goes to the cache owner. Without sending the verification, your credit for the find goes the way of the dodo bird. I did a similar thing with my Classical Cache in Boston, which is a two-stage cache requiring the seeker to bring a knowledge of musical notation, gather information, and send the results back to me. (Told you that I stole this idea.) And, yes, I have deleted claims of a find when I had no e-mail with the correct answers. What can I say? I just work here.

Some virtual caches are placed within view of a Web cam, which periodically takes pictures of the spot. To get credit, you e-mail a copy of the Web page showing you on the spot, usually performing some instruction like holding your GPS receiver up in front of you, so it is obvious that this is not some innocent bystander.

Such virtuals usually require collaboration from someone sitting at a desk. This person monitors the Web cam until an image appears showing you. At that point, the person, in communication with you via a cell phone, saves the Web page for later e-mail delivery to the cache owner. It is theoretically possible to fake this type of image, inserting a picture of yourself in scale into a shot of the empty background, but the amount of work required is far greater than the effort needed to actually get the legitimate image.

For those with a taste for the ultimate in high tech, a number of cell phone service providers, such as Verizon and Sprint PCS, offer wireless Internet service. You can slip an access card into a slot on your laptop, then capture the Web cam image yourself, immediately e-mailing it after for near-instant credit.

Moving

Some caches are virtual; others are physical but move. Someone finding a moving cache generally takes it to a new location. That may be a new spot or one of several in which it is allowed to reside; the rules are at the whim of the cache owner. One moving cache, Keep it Moving, can appear in new places by itself, or be located within other caches, just to keep people on their toes.

The trick in hiding this type of cache is to ensure clear instructions, so that people finding and moving the cache provide the updated location in the place that future seekers will look. Those who find it should follow the directions so other people can enjoy it, too, without taking fruitless trips to find an unexpectedly moved cache.

> **NOTE** Geocaching.com has stopped approving new moving caches, unfortunately, but for good reason. It's tough enough to check that a cache is properly placed once, but as it begins moving, someone might leave it in some inappropriate spot. However, there are still moving caches that were grandfathered in, so get moving and find them.

Hitchhikers and Travel Bugs

Related to the moving cache is the hitchhiker. Instead of the cache moving from place to place, an item moves from one cache to another. In some cases it is just a matter of fun, like The Great Texas-Wisconsin Hitchhiker Races, in which two characters, Butch and Sundance, were racing across multiple states to reach each other's origin. Figure 2-14 shows the page for the first race which, so far as I can tell, is still going on.

Another example of a hitchhiker is the Thoreau Hitchhiker. It's a set of papers that include instructions and coordinates for the actual cache. Part of a finder's responsibility is to remove it from one cache and return it to another in eastern Massachusetts.

A specialized type of hitchhiker is the travel bug. It's actually a pair of metal tags (you buy them at Geocaching.com—hey, they have to make a living somehow) that come with a serial number. You attach one of the tags to some item that can go from one cache to another. In Figure 2-15, you can see two examples: Gwaihir the Windlord, a toy eagle, and Grandpa Bug, a small wrench.

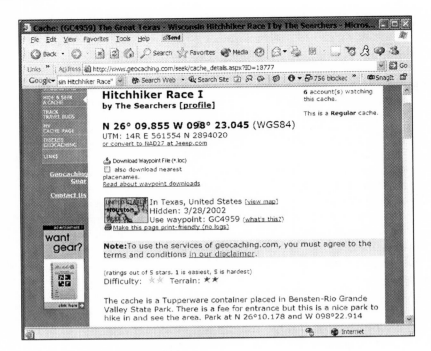

Figure 2-14 Two cache hitchhikers

Figure 2-15 Examples of travel bugs

When you create a travel bug, you keep one of the tags as a record and send the other out into the wild by placing it into a cache. You can also drape the travel bug like a military dog tag identification around the hitchhiker. When finders record the new temporary resting spots on `Geocaching.com` (this doesn't work with `Navicache.com`), the page updates with the number of traveled miles.

As owner of the travel bug, you give its stated mission, which might be something such as visiting a certain number of countries or reaching a particular region that is sunny and warm. One, WitchBlade TB3, named for either the comic book or television show, had the mission to roam the world for a year, traveling to caches "far and wide searching out and destroying evil wherever it is found." We are thankful that the world of geocaching is safer for its existence, even if its namesake television program didn't last beyond a second season.

Benchmarks

Unlike hitchhikers, benchmarks aren't supposed to go anywhere. In fact, they were placed long before geocaching started. These are physical reference marks left by major government survey efforts, and that are now tracked, more or less, by the U.S. National Geodetic Survey (NGS). Typically, these are metal disks set into the ground in plain sight, although most people ignore them.

Although the NGS keeps a database of information on the benchmarks, much of it can be out of date, and the coordinates are often only approximate. So, finding one might be as hard as finding a deliberately hidden cache. What you don't do is take or move one; doing so is a federal crime.

Other organizations, including the U.S. Army Corps of Engineers and the U.S. Bureau of Land Management, place benchmarks. Unfortunately, Geocaching.com doesn't have databases of these (they have only on the NGS variety), and is not set up to handle information on these others. So, if you find a benchmark that doesn't appear on the site, you can't do much with it, other than keep your own tally.

Caching Logistics

You can participate in geocaching just about anywhere you find yourself, because caches exist in nearly 190 countries at the time of writing. But as the Buxley's Geocaching Waypoint world map shows, there are areas of concentration.

You will be busy in the United States, Europe, many parts of Canada, South Africa, and Australia. But there are other regions with some caching presence, like Japan and Malaysia, or parts of Mexico or Brazil. Be aware that cache pages can appear in different languages; I've seen Portuguese and Dutch, but have yet to unearth a subject-appropriate phrase book to decode them. (How do you say Tupperware in German? *Tupperdose*: see the Champagner cache on Geocaching.com.)

Hiding a cache is probably best done during daylight hours so you can easily survey the area for potential issues and problems (see Chapter 7). Finding caches, however, can be a 24-hour-a-day activity. Some seekers head off into the woods with headlamps, flashlights, and more determination than I can generally muster. I'll restrict my nocturnal wanderings to a regular hike in the woods. However, if you do want to give it a shot, Chapter 5 includes some tips on navigating in the physical dark, at least. When it comes to mental dimness, you'll just have to struggle with it yourself, like me.

You can also geocache at almost any time of the year, although you may have to make adjustments to your clothing or travel technique, and certainly give some consideration to leaving an obvious trail to a cache. Some caches may be inaccessible in the winter because of ice or snow. Some may actually be inactive in the summer because of a preponderance of crowds in a given area.

Above everything else, geocaching is a secret activity. You are supposed to hide and find caches without those uninvolved in the activity being alerted to what is happening all around them. This secrecy arises in part from an environmental ethic. One of the early concerns about geocaching is that it would lead to environmental damage, with caches being placed in sensitive areas and searchers beating thousands of unnecessary trails into existing ecosystems. The good news from the land management front is that cachers are being unusually responsible and responsive, working with officials and even carrying out trash left by casual visitors. There's a saying that you'll run into more than once in this book: cache in, trash out.

Before you can trash out, or cache in, or even get close to a cache, you must know the basics of GPS systems, navigation, and hiking. That's what the next few chapters are for.

The Technology

"For a successful technology, reality must take precedence over public relations, for Nature cannot be fooled."—Richard Feynman

Geocaching is one of the few sports that depend on technology. Certainly people could pursue it in a low-tech manner, and those who enjoy scuba diving could switch to snorkeling and simply hold their breaths. Borrowing more heavily from orienteering or letterboxing, significant clues could help direct someone on the hunt to the right spot. But the challenge can be so much greater when you find yourself somewhere within 50 feet of what you seek and all those trees, rocks, and other potential hiding places are taunting you.

If you are going to use technology, it's best to understand how it works to avoid the little misconceptions that can translate to an extra half hour in the snow on a slippery hill. Although by correct choice of caches you can simplify your gadgetary life, you are best prepared by understanding a few things that can aid your search:

- GPS
- Compasses
- Maps
- Altimeters
- Watches
- Radios
- Cell phones

They may seem simple, and they often are, at least as far as a user is concerned. But you may be surprised at how trivial matters will gain in importance the farther you venture from home.

GPS

The GPS is a marvel. The Department of Defense created it to help guide munitions to their destinations; happily, it can also guide you to a cache. But the system does have some significant limitations, and it helps to understand how it works.

The technical name is the Navigation Satellite Timing and Ranging (NAVS-TAR) system. At the heart are 24 satellites in precise orbits that circle the earth twice each day, with a few additional satellites in orbit as back-up units. Each has an atomic clock and runs on solar power. Ground stations, equipped with their own reference paraphernalia, note any position information that seems wrong and feed the corrections back to the satellites. The satellites broadcast a low-power radio signal that provides three sets of information:

- Time, accurate beyond nitpicking

- A special string of numbers that uniquely identifies the satellite

- The updated location of each satellite

The interplay between the ground stations and satellites is accurate, which is fine if that is where you are. But so far, the arrangement does little for people who want to know where they are; that is why GPS receivers exist.

A GPS receiver, or GPSr as we'll call it, is an electronic device that listens to the signals from the satellites, noting the time, identity, and satellite location information. For any given satellite, a receiver can generate the same unique identifying string of numbers.

GPS receivers determine their location through a process called triangulation. Let's start with a two-dimensional analogy. You are out in the country with a view to three landmarks: a water tower, a hill, and a giant tree. You have a map showing all three features and you want to find exactly where on the map you are, as in Figure 3-1.

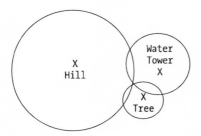

Figure 3-1 Triangulation

Through some minor intervention of technology deities, you find that you are a quarter mile from the tower, a mile from the hill, and 75 feet from the tree. To learn your location, all you have to do is draw three circles on the map that correspond to those distances. The three circles intersect at your location.

GPS Triangulation

Your GPSr is doing something equivalent to the preceding two-dimensional analogy. The differences are that there is no map, the distances involved are on the order of 11,000 miles (the height of the satellites' orbits), and you are dealing with three dimensions instead of two. Each satellite's signal forms a sphere, not a circle, because it extends in all directions. When the spherical signals of two satellites meet, their intersection forms a circle. The sphere of the third satellite intersects that circle in two points, as Figure 3-2 shows. The receiver can determine how far it is from the orbiting satellites and use triangulation to fix its position and, by association, yours.

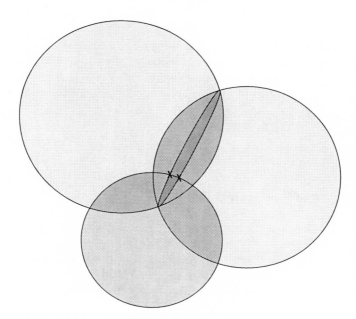

Figure 3-2 Fixing a position by satellite triangulation

Determining those distances precisely enough to be useful is the trick; the corner hardware store is unlikely to have a tape measure that will do. The GPS designers were clever in using a property of physics that people regularly experience. Anyone who watches a baseball game live notices that the bat swings before the crack of wood-on-ball reaches the stands. That is because the image moves at the speed of light while the sound, much slower, arrives later.

Random Talk

The people who designed GPS had to be certain that a receiver would not mistake one satellite for another, which would result in false locations. Having each satellite use a different radio frequency would make receivers more complex to build. An ideal solution would be a series of random numbers: a string of values that cannot be predicted. Unlike the IQ test questions in which someone must look at a series of numbers or objects and determine which comes next, it is impossible to know what the following value should be, which means that it is impossible to generate them on demand. Luckily, there is something called *pseudo-random numbers*. Although not as unpredictable as their cousins, they are "mixed up" enough to make accidental transmission by another source almost impossible, including each other, so all the satellites can use the same frequency without their identifying information becoming scrambled. Computer programs can also create strings of pseudo-random numbers in two different places and have both come out the same, which makes measuring distance possible.

The satellite and receiver generate the same string of numbers at the same time. However, when the satellite's signal reaches the receiver, its copy of the series seems to lag just a little bit, as in Figure 3-3.

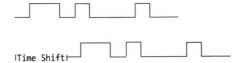

Figure 3-3 Measuring time through signal lag

This occurs because the radio signal must travel the greater than 11,000-mile distance, which, even at the speed of light, takes a noticeable and measurable amount of time. The technical term is that the signals are *out of phase*. By comparing both number series, the receiver calculates how much time the signal took to arrive and, after multiplying by the speed of light (which is how fast radio signals move), the distance from the satellite. So long as the receiver, depending on the unit's manufacturer and model, can obtain the signal from three satellites, you can learn where you are on the planet—more or less. And you thought that this would be simple.

Keeping Time

It sounds good in theory, and works reasonably well in practice, although there is a problem. This scheme assumes that the receiver and the satellites are all on the same time. Remember that the satellites all have incredibly accurate atomic clocks. On the other hand, the receiver must make do with a less accurate clock if its price is to stay under a quarter-million dollars or so. Variations in measuring time can and do create inaccuracies in the positioning calculations. If the clock runs a little fast, the receiver will start its generation of the identity signal a fraction of a second before the satellite does, and the distance will seem longer. Similarly, if the clock is slow, the receiver generates the signal a little after the satellite, and the distance seems shorter. Because the clock will be accurate only within some percentage, all the distances could vary a little, so the point calculated by the receiver could actually be any of many points in a small area, deliberately large in Figure 3-4 to demonstrate the problem.

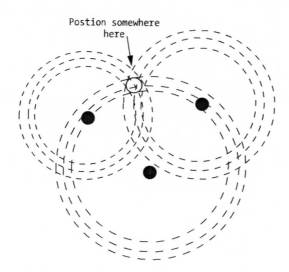

Figure 3-4 Uncertainty of position

If there were only three satellites available, then close would be as good as electronic navigation got. But there are more satellites, and the addition of a fourth nicely solves the timing problem. Going back to Figure 3-4, while the real location is a bit of a question because of the clock's inaccuracy, the receiver doesn't know that. As far as its circuitry can tell, it has delivered the exact spot. Enter the fourth satellite. Suddenly, the receiver has another signal. Because it knows the position information for all the satellites, the GPSr knows where the fourth satellite should be and it calculates the distance. However, the inaccurate clock delivers a different answer. Things are fishy, and those amazing semiconductors rework all the distances and discover what the real time must be. Now the receiver is synchronized with the atomic clocks and can accurately calculate the distances, providing a much more accurate location. That is why all the GPS receivers indicate whether they are locked onto the signals from three satellites or four. Three is the minimum necessary number; if the receiver can only find two satellites, it indicates that there is a problem and will not calculate a position.

The fourth satellite provides yet one more advantage. Three provide what is called a 2D, or two-dimensional, position on the planet's surface. The receiver doesn't have enough information to determine the altitude. With a fourth signal, however, the receiver can give a reasonably good sense of how high up you are with a—you guessed it—3D, or three-dimensional, position, giving your approximate altitude as well as your position on the globe. GPS receivers generally indicate how many satellite signals are locked in at any given time; some also provide a warning when only a 2D positioning is possible. All receivers will tell you when there aren't enough satellite signals available to provide any position at all.

 NOTE The height information is based on a model of what the surface of the earth is supposed to look like. Unfortunately, models are at best approximate, and the estimation of your altitude is notoriously inaccurate.

If you are having trouble visualizing all this, a company called Trimble, which makes GPS devices for surveyors and other commercial users, offers an online GPS tutorial, complete with animations. Visit `http://www.trimble.com/gps` and enjoy the show.

Accuracy

When you look at a display that provides longitude and latitude to an accuracy of three decimal places, there is a temptation to believe that you possess the geographic truth. Realize that no technology is perfect, and that numbers have their limitations.

Ignore the "accuracy" readings on some devices, because you cannot count on them. The GPS promises a horizontal position accuracy of only 15 meters, or a little over 49 feet, and that's *with* the fourth satellite signal. A GPSr may estimate the accuracy of its position calculation, but so many things can affect the results that you can't assume that it is right. Height is even more problematic, and should you get a lock on four satellites, theory says you can only count on being within about 23 meters, or 75 feet of the real altitude. Practice suggests that the accuracy of the calculated height depends on how far apart the satellites are that the receiver has locked onto. The altitude numbers depend on a model of the earth's surface. Models being what they are, the results can vary widely from the actual numbers. In other words, the height can be so far off as to be unusable.

These errors can come from a number of factors. The earlier description of how GPS worked cheated a bit, because it assumes perfect conditions. If you haven't noticed, though, this is not a perfect world. The speed of light is constant in a vacuum, but radio waves actually slow to a degree when they enter the atmosphere. Not only does that affect the timing calculations, which changes distance, but according to physics, the signals bend a little, like light does, distorting things even more. If you are geocaching in a city, you may find that buildings act as mirrors for radio, causing the satellite signals to reflect and appear as though coming from more than one place. This can also happen in heavy forests or woods or in heavy rains: things overhead can cause problems. Even the satellites create some errors: the atomic clocks are not perfect, and minor variations in orbits not caught by the monitoring stations make the positions slightly inaccurate. And the satellite positions heavily influence accuracy. If the signals are coming from a group of satellites that are close together or in a line, the receiver will have trouble determining position very precisely. It's best if, in relation to the receiver, the satellites are at wide angles to each other.

Furthermore, the accuracy in GPS is defined at what is called a 95-percent confidence level, which means that 95 times out of 100, you can expect to be within the given ranges. Those other five times, however, you could end up almost anywhere. Unfortunately, you don't know at the time, or else it would be 100 percent accurate. But then, you are using a GPS receiver to go treasure hunting. Where's the challenge if you know where the cache is every time?

At least the Department of Defense is no longer generally using selective availability, or SA. If you remember the history of GPS, before May of 2000, the military inserted a deliberate error factor that reduced horizontal accuracy to 100 meters, or a little over 300 feet. By the nature of GPS, the vertical error is half again greater, or 150 meters—more than 450 feet. The Department of Defense can turn SA on at any time in the name of national security. Although it seems unlikely, given the amount of civilian business that now relies on the system, should the military feel the need, hopefully it will be after you find that next cache.

Even without SA, military users are at an advantage. GPS satellites transmit not one but two radio signals. Military receivers, and those available to professional users willing to spend the outrageous sums for them, receive both signals, compare them, and correct the results, with a resulting horizontal accuracy of a few feet—at least, that's what the Department of Defense will admit. Civilian units may not use this technology, but there are some other solutions. All the GPS receivers on the market incorporate various techniques to keep problems like multipath errors at a minimum. But that only keeps accuracy to what you would expect.

There is a complex system called differential GPS (DGPS), which your receiver may support. DGPS offers accuracy better than a couple of meters, or six feet—if you have the secondary receivers in fixed positions, which seems like significant fuss for finding a plastic food container hidden in the woods. A solution that sounds more promising is the wide-area augmentation system (WAAS). The Federal Aviation Administration in cooperation with the Department of Transportation is deploying a secondary system of satellites and ground stations to correct the GPS signals for accuracy of three meters/under ten feet. It's currently available only in North America, and even there it's not available everywhere: the satellites are positioned over the equator, so the farther north you are, the harder it is to lock onto the signal, and, boy, can using WAAS eat batteries. Many receivers are WAAS enabled; too bad its usefulness can't be fully realized until future launches of additional satellites.

Choosing a GPSr

You have a wide range of choices in GPS receivers, but not all are a best choice for geocaching. Models specifically intended for mounted use in an automobile or on a boat will generally be too bulky and heavy to hold for extended periods. For geocaching, you want a GPSr intended for handheld use in hiking and backpacking, like the ones in Figure 3-5.

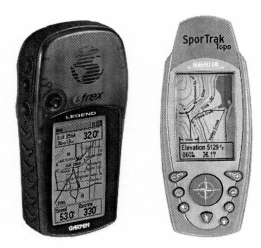

Figure 3-5 Examples of GPS receivers
Photos courtesy of Garmin Ltd. and of Thales Navigation

Garmin, Magellan, and Lowrance have been the three major sources for handheld GPS receivers, and all have models that can work well for geocaching. Brunton, well-known for compasses, also has a handheld GPS. Among perfectly good models for the outdoors, some are better suited to geocaching than others. Then again, personal taste comes into play, as do feature trade-offs. For example, I took a Garmin Legend and a Brunton Multi-Navigator into the field. The Garmin was lighter and graphically displayed my path as I created it—both features I like. But the Brunton offered a larger and easier-to-read screen, and a faster lock on the satellite signals. The story's moral is to check out a variety of units in person, because what pleases one person may leave you cold. This will become evident most strongly with the controls for a given unit. Big buttons? Small buttons? Joysticks? Multiple-choice menus or yes/no step-through operation? Although online ordering may tempt you, trying the receivers is the best course of action; the amount you save could easily be eaten up by aggravation in the field. You can at least get some preliminary research done at OffRoute.com (http://www.offroute.com/comparisons/gps-compare.html).

Standalone GPSr units can also connect by their data cables to a laptop running software like Microsoft Streets & Trips to show your location on a map as you change it. Such companies as Navman, Pharos, and even Magellan also offer units that are really cards plugging into either a laptop or a compatible Pocket PC or Palm-compatible handheld computer. You gain advantages—often a better display and more memory for maps, and general computer capabilities that will let you view a stored Web page or gain wireless connectivity to the Internet (which can be handy, as Chapter 6 explains). But there are prices to pay—in size, weight, and money—if you don't already have the computer. And you can practically watch the battery power shrivel and blow away, which could be a major inconvenience out in the not-so-wild.

For the budget-minded, the more elementary standalone GPS units run about $100, and you can do better with a used model picked up at eBay. A more advanced standalone can run from just under $200 to just under $300, which is roughly the price range for the portable computer add-ons. A high-end GPSr with all the bells and whistles for geocaching can run between $400 and $500.

GPS receivers have their own vocabulary that you should learn before trying to find the model that best suits you and your budget. A common word is *waypoint*, which means a stored location. Every receiver will let you store a waypoint; otherwise, they'd be of little use. Depending on the GPS unit, you may be able to store hundreds of waypoints in memory, though for geocaching purposes, a dozen would suffice. Any receiver you consider must have a *go to* function, in which you choose a waypoint and the device directs you to that location. Some Magellan units has a waypoint averaging feature that takes multiple readings at one location and averages them for an attempt at a more realistic set of coordinates. Some people swear by it, but it's not a must.

Some units let you store collections of waypoints in routes, or paths that you create, going from one waypoint to the next. Such devices will then let you navigate the route, automatically advancing you from one waypoint to the next, and generally they let you flip the route to return to your starting point. For simple geocaching in the local park, you are unlikely to need routes. But as you go on longer hikes, saving a series of waypoints can make it easier to retrace your way back to what passes for civilization. The basic handheld units generally support at least one route.

To follow the directions to a waypoint, GPS units offer some variation on a *directional display*: an arrow directs you to the correct compass point while the receiver displays the amount of distance yet to go. Although this feature falls into the vital category, there are some significant limitations. The directional aspect does not work like a compass, which senses the magnetic field. Instead, the receiver notes your location, the location of the waypoint, and calculates the direction and remaining distance. The receivers do this by examining your locations on a regular basis and determining your direction and speed. But to operate correctly, the receivers need constant movement. When you move too slowly (under two miles an hour), the directional feature loses its orientation and can actually point in the wrong direction. One feature in many receivers is cross-track error (XTE), which allows an estimation of how far you are deviating from the most direct path to your destination waypoint. Although useful for planes and boats, this ends up being of virtually no value on foot, because too often you cannot take a straight-line approach.

This is why carrying a compass is important (to be covered later in this chapter and in Chapter 4, which discusses navigation). That is why you also want a *track log* feature. Instead of calculating only a running estimation of your direction and speed, a track keeps your actual progress; in some cases, the GPSr can graphically display the track. The latter is a fabulous feature for getting yourself un-lost, and the next chapter covers its use.

Tracks are also marvelous when combined with another feature: *mapping*. A number of GPS models have some amount of land and even sea detail stored, and these generally allow you to download detailed maps, both topographic (the type used in wilderness navigation) and street, from compatible software. Combining mapping with tracks lets you see your progress in relation to the downloaded map. This is not a must-have, but falls into the "really nice and I hope someone buys me one" category.

To download a map, you need a GPS that can connect to your computer. All the units I've seen do this, but be sure to acquire the appropriate cable if the receiver does not include it (not all do). Electronic communications are a two-way street, and this will also allow you to upload waypoints, routes, and tracks, incorporating your treks with the appropriate topographic map. If there is an area you often hike and you have topographic map software, you can track your walks along the trails and upload them, so you create your own private trail guide integrated with a topographic map.

Downloading maps to GPS units means *memory*, and a lot more than you might think; you can easily use up 8MB. Garmin handheld units tend to have only the memory that comes built-in, but Lowrance and Magellan let you add memory with slip-in cards.

Go for a receiver that can offer at least *12-channel parallel reception*. That means the GPSr can check signals from multiple satellites all at the same time, rather than getting a fix on one, then moving to another and yet another. This feature is easy to find. Although WAAS doesn't work well in many places, it can be useful and is worth having if you aren't paying a premium. You want a back-light on the display for those times that you are geocaching late or in a shaded area. A good option is a car power adapter (for the drive to the location—and, yes, you'll be using the GPSr then) and maybe a vehicle mounting bracket, so you don't have the unit sliding about on the dashboard and potentially bouncing out a window.

The receiver should support a variety of map grids and datums (more on both in the next chapter). Of the latter, your device should literally support dozens of country-specific options as well as World Geodetic System 1984 (WGS84), an international standard for map information. Grids should include UTM, latitude/longitude, MGRS, and any other country-specific ones that you might need.

You want a waterproof case. No, you have no intention of dropping your GPS or using it in . . . moist conditions. Get a waterproof unit anyway; you might be surprised. There are different ratings bandied about: IEC-529 IPX7 and IP65 are two I've come across. The first means the unit can be held at a meter, or just over a yard, underwater for 30 minutes, and the latter guarantees only 10 minutes at half that distance. What may not be clear is that the waterproofing may not extend to the battery case. If you drop your waterproof receiver in the water, you should dry it, then remove the batteries and dry that compartment.

And keep plenty of spare batteries. The handheld models I've seen and researched have battery life estimates of roughly 14 to 20 hours. However, that measurement is generally made in some kind of power-saving mode, in which the unit samples its position less frequently. That should be fine—how fast do you walk, anyway?

Some of the available devices are just GPS receivers; others, like the Brunton Multi-Navigator and the Garmin eTrex Vista, incorporate digital compass and barometric altimeter. The Garmin Rhino series combines GPS receiver with two-way radio, so you can talk to other members of your geo-caching party, should you get separated. These units also transmit your location to others in your party so they can find you.

Compasses

When it works (batteries good, clear view to the sky), a GPSr admirably performs its function of providing a position. Nevertheless, even under the best conditions, it is easy to get lost with a GPSr, because there is more to finding your way than knowing your position. You must place that position in the context of its surroundings and orient yourself to the direction in which you want to travel. If you are standing still, or even moving too slowly, a GPSr cannot help with orientation.

This is why it always makes sense to take a compass with you. I don't mean one of those dial compasses that you might find in a box of cereal, but the type meant to be used in the wild with a map. Figure 3-6 shows an example of this type of compass.

Compasses work today just the same as they have through the ages: a magnetized piece of metal is allowed to rotate freely. It orients itself to the magnetic field of the earth, pointing north. Compasses can work indoors or out, in good and bad weather, although metal objects too close can throw off their operation.

The compass shown in Figure 3-6 is actually a baseplate compass, which is the best type for general navigation, as far as I'm concerned. On the plate are scales that can measure distances on standard types of topographic maps. Around the compass face is a bezel, or dial, marked with the 360° found in a circle. The degree markings represent *azimuth*, which is a way of referring to directions in relation to north. If north is at the top of a circle that is divided into degrees, any other direction is equivalent to some other position on the circle. That other direction's azimuth is the corresponding degree mark. For example, east has an azimuth of 90°, because it is found 90° from north on the circle. South falls 180°; west is 270°. The azimuth of 135° corresponds to southwest. Note that although *azimuth* is the correct term, hikers often interchangeably use the term *bearing*, although with a bearing (used with UTM), the degree reading is book-ended by cardinal directions. So an azimuth of 135 corresponds to the bearing E 135 S. But if you see the two words treated as identical in outdoor literature, don't let it throw you. Appropriately enough, the bezel is called the azimuth ring, as you can see in Figure 3-7.

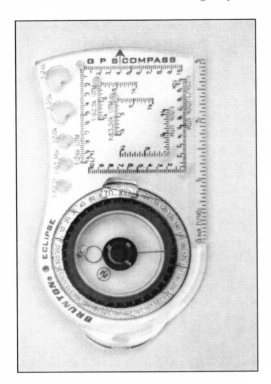

Figure 3-6 Example of a compass

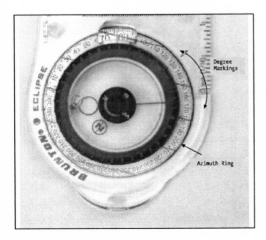

Figure 3-7 Azimuth ring

The azimuth ring can turn. Inside the compass's face is an orienting arrow that turns with the ring. Another arrow on the baseplate is fixed. This arrangement, which the next chapter describes in detail, lets you determine the azimuth of anything around you, and also allows you to move between your surrounds and a topographic map, so you can find where you are and where you are going. This type of compass is often called an orienteering compass, because of its popularity for that racing navigation sport.

An excellent compass feature is an adjustment for an error factor called *magnetic declination*. Magnetic north is actually off from true north (the top of the earth). Depending on where you are on the planet, the arrow that spins and points to magnetic north can be a good 15° to 20° off from true north, as in Figure 3-8.

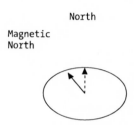

Figure 3-8 Magnetic declination

If you are trying to work with a map whose reference is true north, magnetic declination can get you seriously off track. (If you are only using the compass to find azimuths and don't have a map handy, you can work without a problem.) A magnetic declination adjustment can take this factor into account without the need for you to remember whether you need to add or subtract the declination. (Again, there is more about all this in the next chapter.)

An additional good feature is a mirror; it lets you accurately line up the orienting arrow with the compass arrow while you point the compass at some object, allowing easier and more accurate navigation. A clinometer is yet another arrow in the compass housing (and in the navigation quiver) that lets you determine angles of slopes and heights of objects. It can do some solid work in scoping out a leg of a hike or in placing yourself on a map, and also plays an important part in bragging rights. ("You wouldn't believe the slope of that last hill," he said, gazing through the smoke of the bar and tipping back a beer.)

One thing to remember about compasses is that they are designed for certain areas of the planet. There is a second property that concerns compasses, called *magnetic inclination*. Because the earth is curved, so is its magnetic field. An angle exists between the field and the horizontal plane in which most of us live, and that is the magnetic inclination. Its effect is to pull a compass needle down, and not just around. The magnetic inclination, or dip, can cause the needle to bind and give inaccurate readings. Compass manufacturers balance needles so that they turn easily in particular areas of the world, typically in either the northern or southern hemisphere over a range of three to five time zones. If using a compass outside of its intended zone of operation, test it in an area like a city where you can easily verify compass directions against a street map and see how it works. If you will be traveling far and plan to geocache (and you can almost anywhere on the planet), you can order a compatible compass from any manufacturer. Be sure to label it before you head off, or you might mix your compasses. There are some models designed to work anywhere on the planet, but they will be more expensive and, according to some experts, more fragile than the regular type.

Digital compasses are also available—some built into GPS receivers, some separate devices, and still others built into watches and combined with altimeters. They are fine, but the consumer versions are, perhaps contrary to expectations, not more accurate than the traditional type. Also, I find a regular compass with a sight easier to use in shooting azimuths (again, more in the next chapter), and the digital type are virtually useless in conjunction with a topographic map. However, not all navigation has to be done with a map; you can get along well enough in many public forests and mountains with compass azimuths and a notebook to keep pertinent details of your walk. If you might use a map, though, then stick with what works.

Prices for a usable compass start at about $15 and can rise to $80, with the additional cost bringing more features and greater built-in versatility in using maps of different scale. Because I favor traditional compasses, I have models from Brunton and Suunto, both highly reputable manufacturers. Another name is Silva (though it's sold under the Brunton name in the United States and Canada).

Maps

In any hiking out in the wild, a map is an absolute necessity. Many places that house geocaches are so close to "civilization" that a map is less necessary. One can still be useful for doing research prior to seeking or hiding a cache; one geocacher in my area is notorious for not using a GPSr, but instead for doing extensive research with topographic maps and even aerial photography. Maps become increasingly necessary as you stray from the spots within close access to roads and buildings.

Every country or region will have its own source of maps. In the United States, topographic maps can come from a number of sources, including the U.S. Geological Survey (USGS), the U.S. Forest Service (for national forests), the National Park Service (for national park maps), or the Bureau of Land Management, although retail outdoor or map stores may be faster ways of obtaining what you want. Canada's source for topographic maps is the Centre for Topographic Information. The United Kingdom has its Ordnance Survey, and France its Institut Geographique National (IGN). Check with local outdoor stores, the chains like REI and EMS (why do the outdoors attract three-letter acronyms?), or online sources. A few software packages are available that let you pick a spot and print a custom topographic map. Check the resources appendix for some suggestions.

Every topographic map has a map datum and a grid. The map datum is the set of reference information upon which the map is based. The world of GPS uses a datum called WGS 84. Many topographic maps, however, were created long before the creation of WGS 84. In the United States, for example, maps often use the North American Datum 1924 (NAD24), although newer maps use the North American Datum 1983 (NAD83), which is actually the same as WGS 84. There are many other datums around the world.

The grid is the set of coordinates that let you find positions on the map. The grid system most familiar to you may be latitude and longitude (lat/lon), where positions are expressed in degrees. But one you should learn about is the previously described UTM. Instead of degrees, UTM describes every point as a set of distances from two reference locations, all expressed in metric units. Geocaching sites give both coordinate types for any geocache. You can use whichever you find more comfortable, but there is an advantage to learning UTM: you can calculate distances easily. (Yes, it's another topic for Chapter 4.)

One thing to keep in mind, however, is that the coordinates on the geocaching sites are all given using the WGS 84 datum. If you want to find the cache on a map using a different datum, say NAD24, then you need to convert whatever coordinates you use—whether lat/lon or UTM—because the same coordinates under the different datums can differ by more than one-tenth of a mile, or close to 170 meters. The resources appendix can direct you to some Web sites that can help. You will also need to set your GPSr to use the right datum, to say nothing of coordinate system.

Many maps come folded for easy storage and use. Many others arrive as flat sheets, so you should learn some basic map-folding techniques.

The first technique makes your map look like any fold-out version you get to keep in your auto. Place the map on a flat surface with the top facing away from you and the printed side facing up. Fold the right side over to the left, making a sharp crease, and then unfold it again. (See Figure 3-9.)

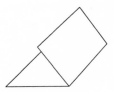

Figure 3-9 First step of map folding

Next, fold both edges to meet in the middle. Take the two edges and fold them backward to start the accordion pleat shown in Figure 3-10.

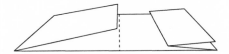

Figure 3-10 Second step of map folding

Flip the map over, take the two sides and fold them back to the middle. Now you can flip the map back, fold it in half, and then fold into thirds for easy storage, as Figure 3-11 shows.

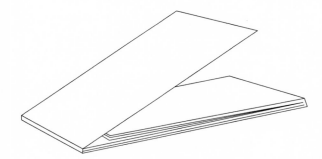

Figure 3-11 Third step of map folding

The next three techniques are often mentioned on Web sites that cover map folding. The diagrams often look identical because they are almost inevitably taken from a public domain work, "Map Reading and Land Navigation," from the Department of Defense. In the first one, you place the map with the top facing away from you, but this time you place the map printed side down. Fold the map in half with the print facing out. Fold the map into quarters, as in Figure 3-12, and then fold the edges back into an accordion shape.

Figure 3-12 Another accordion fold

A simpler way is to fold the map in half as in the last approach, and then into thirds. Figure 3-13 shows the final fold in half.

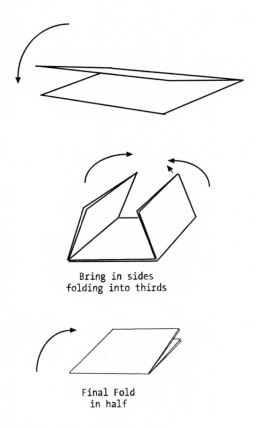

Bring in sides
folding into thirds

Final Fold
in half

Figure 3-13 A third map fold

Finally comes a really clever preparation. A single cut in the center of the map allows an ingenious set of folds that lets you flip map segments back and forth, providing access to any section that you wish while leaving it compact for easy storage and carrying, as you can see in Figure 3-14.

Wet conditions outdoors are common, and dealing with a mass of wet paper is no fun, so you want your map to remain unaffected. You can achieve this in several ways. One is to keep the map in a waterproof container. One of the freezer bags can do wonders, especially if you fold the map so that the part you want to see faces out. Heavier and more durable commercial map cases are available at outdoor retailers. However, accounting for the difference in price, it might be cheaper to use a succession of Ziploc bags. You can also buy waterproofing solution to spread on maps; Stormproof, Aquaseal, and Nikwax are all available brands.

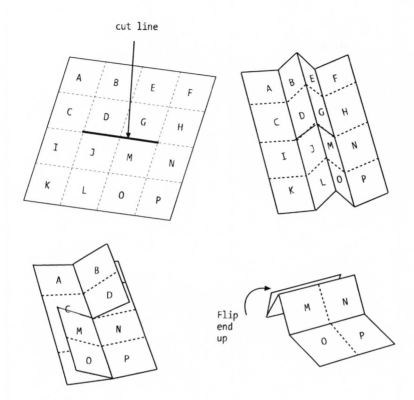

Figure 3-14 A compact map preparation

Portable Computing

Some people love bringing other advanced gadgets on geocaching excursions. Handheld computers, either Pocket PC or Palm, can store maps. More importantly, they can display Web pages, which means that a device such as that in Figure 3-15 can save the cache description as well as hints and read them. There is also a special service for paying members on Geocaching.com that allows you to collect cache information and download it to one of these devices.

Figure 3-15 Handheld computer
Photo courtesy of Hewlett-Packard Company

You could also just print out the page and fold it up. But the paper won't connect wirelessly to the Internet, should you get the urge to do some online research to help you in your hunt. Don't laugh. I can remember being out on a search in a forest in which my receiver wasn't working well. A hint said to look for the two giant beech trees, then to travel past the giant hemlock tree. Hemlock? Isn't that what Socrates had to drink when he was committed to death? I was feeling flora-challenged. Being able to point a browser to `Google.com` and search for a picture of a hemlock would have shown both the poisonous herb and the evergreen tree with its distinctively rough bark. And even though the GPS signal bounced off the coniferous landscape, cell phone signals worked admirably well, so there would have been the opportunity for a wireless Internet connection to come in handy.

Because driving to the parking spots can be as tricky as finding the cache, some people mount a laptop on the dashboard that displays a map and often incorporates a GPS card for the computer equivalent of "You are here." (Some people do serious driving to go geocaching.)

Talk about overkill. To quote the fine outdoor author Colin Fletcher: my technological God.

Altimeters

A GPSr can give you a reading on how high you are above sea level, but the number is of questionable accuracy even if you do have a lock on four satellites. Drop down to three, and you won't have a clue. Although knowing your altitude with precision probably best serves curiosity when in the local outdoor recreation level, if you go for caches in more remote locations, reliable height information can make it easier to place yourself on a map.

In that case, consider buying an altimeter. They work on barometric pressure, and so usually include a barometer reading. (See Figure 3-16.)

Figure 3-16 Altimeter
Photo courtesy of Brunton

Altimeters are often built into special watches or may be included with a digital compass or even in a GPSr. There are even pocket knives with altimeters. You can easily spend $150 or more for a watch with an altimeter that can show altitude to a 10-foot or better accuracy.

Realize, however, that this is something requiring daily calibration; otherwise, a pressure change resulting from weather patterns can suddenly make your height appear to change. Someone at a local EMS store told me that the altimeters in the display case, which were not regularly calibrated, would display altitudes that could shift as much as 700 feet from one day to the next. If you use one, you will either need a reference height or a reference barometric pressure at sea level. If out on a multiday trip, record the altitude at your camp site on paper. That way, you can recalibrate the next morning without having to radio for meteorological help.

Two-Way Radios

Speaking of radios, if you are out with a group of people, there is a type of consumer two-way radio called family radio service (FRS). These radios don't need a license and can communicate up to two miles, if there are no obstructions. In other words, one mile may be the best you get in practical application. However, that can be good enough to help keep your group together. My family has even used such radios to keep an eye, or ear, on the kids at the annual town fair.

Figure 3-17 FRS radio
Photo courtesy of Motorola, Inc. Motorola Inc. and/or Giant International are not
responsible for misrepresentation and/or fraudulent use of photo

You can find FRS radios at most consumer electronics stores. They provide up to 14 channels of communication, so you don't get interference with
other radio users, and they also have privacy codes to keep your talk to your
group. Pairs of decent radios will start in the $40 to $50 range and run up to
about $100.

Don't be confused by the availability of general mobile radio service
(GMRS). Although you can purchase GMRS radios as easily as FRS models
(or devices that include both), you need a Federal Communications
Commission (FCC) license to use the former. Such a license that covers your
family costs $80 for five years, and that does nothing for friends going geo-
caching. The advantage is that the GMRS radios are more powerful and can
transmit over a longer distance. But I'm not sure that it's worth the licensing
fee, given the type of use in geocaching. Be aware that many consumer stores
selling two-way radios don't understand the difference between the services
and will know nothing of license requirements. Just do the homework for
them. If the radio has an output power of .5 watts, it's FRS and you are clear
to use it. If the output is higher, it's GMRS, and you shouldn't buy it unless
you are getting an FCC license.

Cell Phones

Surely I must jest. Virtually everyone in the world has been exposed, if not overexposed, to the ubiquitous communication devices that are disturbingly reminiscent of the communicators once used on the television show *Star Trek*. Flip open the case, punch some buttons, and you can connect to almost anywhere in the world.

Unfortunately, cell phones have some significant restrictions that can cause problems, particularly out in the woods. The phones rely on cellular towers: central antennas that note the presence of phones, accept transmissions from them, relay the content to the telephone system, and similarly pass on the response from the phone on the other end.

The usefulness of a phone in a given geographic area depends completely on how well represented in the region the company is that provides cellular service to that device. A provider might have good coverage in one spot and poor service in another, and the user might find the phone useless in some locales.

In most of life, being out of touch is nothing but an annoyance. Such a temporary outage displays a different character when your health and safety are involved. Furthermore, calling for help should be the ultimate last resort. Asking for people to rescue is also asking them to inconvenience themselves and perhaps put them in danger. North of me in New Hampshire, for example, authorities field hundreds of calls from wayward hikers. So many walked into the mountains with blissful disregard for reality that the state has authorized fines for those who call for aid after exercising their rights to be foolish.

So don't be foolish, and do learn what to do when you are lost in the woods.

Lost in Style

"I have never been lost, but I will admit to being confused for several weeks."—Daniel Boone

It is disconcerting to be in the woods and suddenly realize that you haven't a clue as to where you are or how to get to where you are going. As I've learned, it is additionally embarrassing when you are only a few minutes by foot from your home. Even relatively small patches of public conservation land, bounded on all sides by roads, houses, and other implements of civilization, can seem like impenetrable wilderness that will consume your existence, or at least delay dinner. I can remember plunging along a "shortcut" in pursuing a cache and confusedly wandering about for a good hour or more.

If navigation is a basic skill for hikers, kayakers, rock climbers, and scuba divers, it is elemental for geocaching; after all, the entire point is to find a specific place. As the great pioneer Daniel Boone, who went on his last hunting trip at age 83, could attest, anyone can become disoriented. Ironically, becoming lost with a GPS receiver in hand is easier than finding dirt. That is because many people use GPS without employing other useful navigation tools and skills.

This one chapter won't show you every skill possible for land navigation. What it will provide is the essential knowledge for helping you be comfortable in most of the situations geocaching will put upon you. For the more difficult and extreme caches hidden far from populated areas, I have listed several specialized books on navigation in the resources appendix. I've read them all and found that their information does overlap, but be warned: each book covers topics or techniques not found in the others. To be thorough, you will find yourself reading more than one.

Lost and Found

The world teaches that being lost or found is something absolute: either you are one or the other. However, think of driving home from work: you know the way, but if part of your route fell on a featureless highway, you might be hard pressed to stop and find the exact spot on a map. Nevertheless, you still wouldn't feel lost even though you did not know precisely where you were. Your knowledge of the drive to your home on the East Coast would prove virtually useless should you need to travel to Walla Walla, Washington.

So being lost is a relative condition. You want to ensure that, while geocaching, waywardness is a poor cousin thrice removed. This approach will let you get to caches and back home (or to other caches) more quickly. Knowing where you are consists of three components:

- Position

- Orientation

- Intended direction

Position is the knowledge of your location with respect to your surroundings with a degree of precision that meets your requirements. A mouthful of words to be sure, and seemingly as vague as a politician's promise, but actually surprisingly useful. A GPSr can generally indicate your position within 15 meters, or 50 feet on the high end, and often is accurate to 10 meters, or 30 feet—sometimes even closer. This precision is an astonishing technical feat, and useful. But that information is completely useless if you are standing confused in the middle of a sea of forest, if you will pardon my temporarily mixed terrains of metaphor. Accurate numbers do nothing for you unless you know that they mean you are about a quarter mile from a cache and a five-minute walk up the trail from your car.

Knowing your position doesn't guarantee knowing your orientation, which is your alignment with your surroundings. When you approach an intersection in your town, you know which way to turn because you are familiar with the area and know that a right will take you to the river, and to your left is a shopping district. In the woods, though, you may not have that practiced degree of orientation. Take that walk up the path to the cache, find it, then start heading back to your car. If you come to a trail intersection, you cannot pick the correct branch—even if you have a map—without proper orientation, because you don't know if you are turning east toward the hills or west to the parking lot.

Intended direction is the way in which you want to travel. A compass and GPS can provide a location and orientation that can be transferred to a map. None of this will do much good if the mapped area is totally covered by forest and you don't know in which direction you need to walk to reach the cache— or your automobile and dinner. (See Figure 4-1.)

See? It says that we're right here - again.

Figure 4-1 Losing your direction

For those of you still more comfortable with urban analogies, say you find yourself on Broadway in Manhattan. The street runs roughly uptown and downtown, and you have tickets to a musical. You need to know the nearest numerical cross-street, which provides position; how the cross-streets run higher and lower in sequence, so you can determine your orientation; and the cross-street at which you can find the theater, which suggests an obvious direction.

If any one of these positioning factors is inaccurate, you will be lost. For example, if you don't know the theater's cross-street, you don't know where you need to go. Oh, you might find it, but you will undoubtedly do a lot of walking to check all the possibilities. If you have the theater's location but don't know which way the streets run, you don't know the theater's position relative to your own. And without knowing your position on Broadway, you don't know whether you have enough time to walk or if you should hail a cab to make the curtain. So, relative to the woods, you need to know where you are on a trail, which way you want to go, and what turns to take or avoid.

Whether in the city or country, losing your grasp on any of the three positioning factors could send the others tumbling. If you start with the wrong position, your orientation is nonexistent. When orientation goes, direction to your goal is soon to follow. Pursuing the wrong place makes your position and orientation only good for slinking back to the car with your tail between your legs.

Geocaching navigation is accomplished in a variety of ways. Some people simply follow the GPSr to the cache's waypoint. Others eschew technology. Someone who lives near me has found well over 1,200 caches (at the time of writing) without using a GPSr by enthusiastically employing only maps, aerial photography, clues left by the cache owner, and a willingness to spend significant time searching. To my thinking, a combination of the different methods is advisable. But to use any of these tools together or apart, you must know how they describe the world, which means you must understand grids.

Coordinate Grids

For geocaching to work, people who hide caches must be able to communicate their locations to those who seek caches. Fortuitously, there is a mechanism for doing so: a grid. Several types exist, but all grids are essentially the same in concept; they specify a point by giving its north/south and east/west positions. By using grids, you can find caches, tell people where to find the ones that you have hidden, and move from GPSr to map to compass and back again.

Although there are different grids for different needs, geocaching uses two: latitude/longitude (lat/lon) and Universal Transverse Mercator (UTM).

Latitude and Longitude

You are probably familiar with the terms *latitude* and *longitude*. Both are types of coordinates that, together, specify a grid for the globe. In this case, the coordinates are angular in nature. Remember that a circle is 360° around, and a globe is no more than a collection of circles. Latitude is the collection of circles that lie parallel to the equator, and longitude represents the half circles passing through the north and south poles, as Figure 4-2 shows.

Latitude lines may run east and west, but are really a measure of north/south position, because they are circles defined as all the points at a certain distance north or south of the equator. The equator represents 0° latitude. All other lines of latitude run up to 90° north, toward the North Pole, or down to 90° south toward the South Pole.

The references for all longitude lines is the half circle passing through both poles as well as Greenwich, England (0° longitude) and the other half circle, on the opposite side of the globe, passing through the poles and the International Date Line in the Pacific Ocean (180° longitude). All other longitudes are expressed in degrees from 0 to 180 and as east or west of Greenwich.

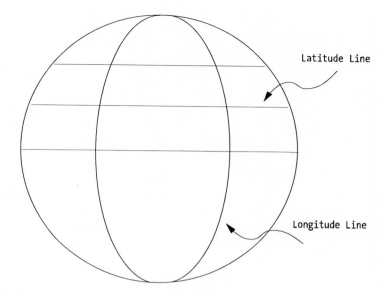

Figure 4-2 Latitude and longitude

Latitude and longitude are expressed as angular measurements; a combination of degrees, minutes (60 to the degree), and seconds (60 to the minute) describe your location, as Figure 4-3 shows. As an example, the Eiffel Tower in Paris has a latitude of 48°51'32"N (48 degrees, 51 minutes, 32 seconds north) and a longitude of 002°17'35"E (2 degrees, 17 minutes, 35 seconds east).

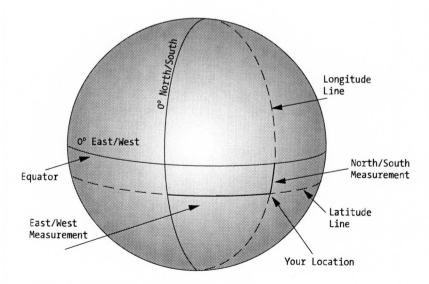

Figure 4-3 Angular measurements of your location

Because lines of longitude converge as they approach the north and south poles, the distance between any two decreases the farther north (or south) that you go. Two lines of latitude, being parallel, always remain the same distance apart. This may seem like a flashback to high school geometry, but these are important facts because you can actually find a cache's location on a topographic map with a special ruler that measures degrees and that is designed for the scale of your map, which you'll find out about later in this chapter.

Many geocachers are comfortable with lat/lon, but there are some advantages to dealing with caching life through the linear measurements of UTM.

Universal Transverse Mercator (UTM)

Remember from the last chapter that in UTM, the world is split into 60 zones, numbered from 1 to 60, bounded by longitudinal lines separated by 6°, as shown in Figure 4-4. Zone 1 starts at 180° longitude. Each of the zones has a middle line, called the zone meridian, that is 3° from either side of the zone.

World Divided into 60 UTM zones

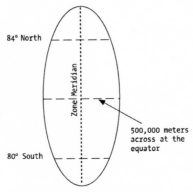

A single UTM slice, 6 degrees wide

Figure 4-4 UTM system of measurement

UTM flattens out these zones, which distorts things a bit, but not usually enough to be a problem. Where distortion does become a problem is the regions above the 84° northern latitude line and below the 80° southern latitude line. As a result, those areas do not appear as part of the UTM scheme of things. This shouldn't matter, because little geocaching occurs in the Arctic and Antarctic.

> **NOTE** I say little, because at the time of this writing, there were ten caches in Antarctica and a few in the Arctic Circle. There are some people who will geocache anywhere.

UTM works with linear measurements: an *easting* that identifies the horizontal (east/west) position, and a *northing* for the vertical (north/south). For each zone, there are two references for these measurements: the zone meridian for the easting and the equator for the northing.

At the equator, a zone is 1,000 kilometers (about 620 miles) wide, so the zone meridian has an easting of 500 kilometers, or 500,000 meters, as shown in Figure 4-4. Within a zone, the eastings to the west of the meridian are smaller than 500,000 meters; those to the east are larger.

As for northings, those in the northern hemisphere use the equator as a zero point, so the northing is the distance north of the equator. For the southern hemisphere, however, the equator lies at 10,000,000 meters, and so a northing is 10,000,000 minus the distance from the given point to the equator.

If it sounds confusing, just ignore it, because when you look at an actual topographic map, it all becomes easy. A set of UTM coordinates, in this case for the Eiffel Tower, will look something like 31 E 448147 N 5412010. On maps, you might find the easting shown as 448^{147} and the northing as 5412^{010}. The superscript numbers are just a formatting convention—I guess to make them easier to read—and has no influence on their meaning. Sometimes you will see something that seems like UTM coordinates that start with a letter code, like 19T E 343078 N 4685350, which happen to be the coordinates of the first cache I hid. These are actually the U.S. Military Grid Reference System, or MGRS. The letters indicate horizontal bands 8° in height stacked north to south. They start with C, which extends from 80° south latitude (lowest point in UTM or MGRS) to 72° south, and omitting I and O, they go up to X, which is north 72° to north 84°. Notice that band X is actually 12°; this is because there are a total of 164°, not counting the areas that UTM and MGRS don't cover, and something must cover the extra four degrees. So the T indicates roughly what north/south part of the zone contains the coordinate. (See Figure 4-5.)

UTM has some significant advantages over lat/lon. One is that by comparing two UTM coordinates (like that of a cache and your current location, according to your GPS), you can always determine which is farther east or farther north: the larger easting value is always farther east, and the larger northing value is always farther north. Finding the distance between two points is a matter of high school geometry, as Figure 4-6 shows.

The difference between the easting and northing values helps form a right triangle. By using the Pythagorean theorem that the square of the hypotenuse (long side) of a right triangle is the sum of the squares of the sides, you can find the distance between the two points. Using a calculator, square the difference between the eastings and the difference between the northings. Add the two results and then take the square root.

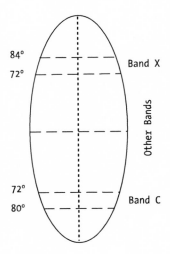

Figure 4-5 UTM grid

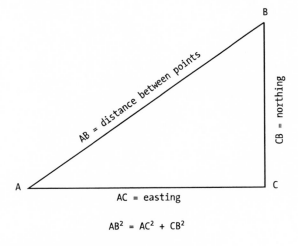

$$AB^2 = AC^2 + CB^2$$

Figure 4-6 A trip down mathematical memory lane

Although you could jump right to discussing how to use coordinates with a GPSr so you can immediately seek your first cache, it can be useful to first look at grids in relation to maps—to put the whole world, so to speak, into perspective.

Maps

Maps are excellent navigational aids because they can offer a summary of position, orientation, and direction at one time. You can research a potential destination, follow your progress, and find your way back. They also offer a delicate beauty born of utility, mathematical principle, and artistic merit. For those unimpressed by subtlety, they can keep you from wandering about in circles for several hours.

Three types of maps may prove useful to you. To drive to the general cache location, a *street map* can work wonders. Following the direct-line directions of a GPSr when driving on an unforgiving grid of city and town streets is difficult at best. When you undertake your pre-hunt research (see Chapter 4), you will check the general vicinity online. Taking that knowledge and applying it to a street map as you drive can save half the time of your total hunt. (So I exaggerate; it just *feels* like half the time.)

A *trail map*, on the other hand, is exactly what its name suggests: a map of walking or biking trails in a particular area. If you can find one for the area holding the cache, it can save you time in finding the best route to the cache and any route back to your vehicle.

For the actual walking, I also like to use a *topographic map*, mentioned in the previous chapter, and a trail map. Figure 4-7 shows an example of a topographic map.

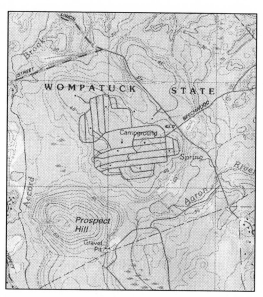

Figure 4-7 Topographic map

The size of the book limits what you can see, so pick up a topographic map (available at an outdoor or map store) and look at the following features:

1. Title: This tells the area covered by a map and is the way you indicate which one you want. You must find the proper map covering the area with the cache. The U.S. Geological Survey has a free index of the maps. Map software eliminates the problem, allowing you to specify custom slices. (See Appendix A for more on this.)

2. Datum: The map will indicate which mass of cartographic information formed its basis. Identical coordinates on two seemingly similar maps using different data can vary by hundreds of meters, or even more feet.

3. Grid or grid tick marks: They are the coordinates you use to pinpoint a spot on the map.

4. Contour lines and index contour lines: Show the approximate height of any point on the map. The index contour lines appear as every fifth contour line, and they have their height marked on the map to make calculations easier.

5. Contour interval: This is the height difference between any two adjacent contour lines.

6. Map date: A critical consideration often overlooked, the map date shows the last year during which the map was checked for accuracy. A map with a date from the late 1920s may well miss many roads and other features that would be present on a more contemporary issue.

7. Grid and north orientation: As you will see later in this chapter, there is a difference between true north and magnetic north, and in some cases, the top of the map is actually different from both of them. By checking the relative differences, you can know how to adjust between a compass, a GPSr, and a map.

8. Legend: Don't know whether the line you are looking at is a contour or a road? Check the legend, which is a listing of the different marks you might see on the map and what they mean.

9. Landmarks: Typical things that appear on a map are such landmarks as schools, churches, public buildings, and houses.

The contour lines are one major advantage of a topographic map. Each line indicates a particular elevation above sea level and represents a path that remains completely flat, going neither uphill nor down, if you walked it. Following a contour is a good, although not perfect, indication that you are taking a relatively easy route. This approach is imperfect because there is only so much detail a topographic map can show. Say that the contour lists a particular elevation at 180 feet and that the contour interval is 30 feet. (Substitute meters if it makes you more comfortable.) There can still be changes in height of less than 30 feet that aren't large enough to warrant a note on the map. So getting from point A to point B might require you to climb a 10-foot vertical rise, as Figure 4-8 shows.

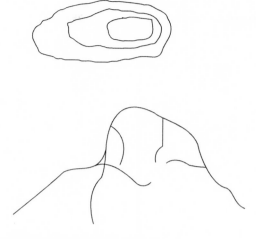

Figure 4-8 Unexpected heights between contours

The contours also do not reveal the nature of the walking surface. I recently bushwhacked up a hill with my son. Normally, this would require significant effort, but the area had just seen a fair snowfall, and the bramble, sticks, and other snares were safely blanketed, making the ascent relatively easy. For the most part, topographic maps are usually reliable—though anyone who has used them enough knows the feeling of suddenly finding that a listed road or feature does not exist. Cartographers, it seems, are only human.

By counting contours, you can find the difference in height between any two points. In Figure 4-9, point A is at 50 meters, or just under 164 feet, because it is an index contour line marked as 50. Point B is at 80 meters, or about 262 feet, because it is three lines over from A and the height difference between the contour index lines is 50 meters. That means that A and B differ in altitude by 30 meters, or 98 feet. To determine whether you will walk uphill or down, examine the way the contour values change.

You can find the distance between any two points (A and B, if you can believe it) by measuring the distance on the map and comparing that to the scale on the map's legend. You might encounter several of these common scales: 1:24,000, 1:25,000, and 1:62,500. So each inch represents 24,000 inches in the first scale, 25,000 in the second, and 62,500 in the third. For metric measurements, 1 centimeter becomes 24,000, and so on. To make this a little more comprehensible, on a 1:25,000 scale, an inch represents about .4 miles; a centimeter is about 800 meters. There are larger scales—1:150,000 and 1:250,000 for example—but it's best to avoid them because they probably won't show details that could come in handy.

With some practice, you'll find that contour lines also reveal much about the appearance of the land the map represents. The closer the lines are, the more height is gained over a given distance, and so the steeper the slope. By looking at the patterns, you can relate—that is, orient—the map to the surroundings. Figure 4-10 shows some examples of how topographic drawings correspond to actual landscape features.

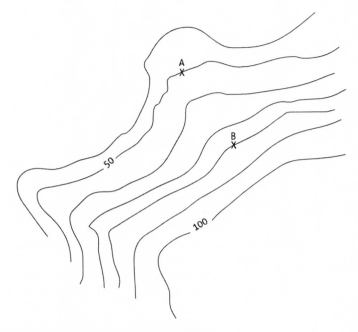

Figure 4-9 Using contours to determine height

In addition to finding the difference in height between two points, you can use a ruler with the map to discover the linear distance between them. The map has a scale showing how to translate a linear distance on paper to the actual distance on land. Measure the distance between the two points on the map, then use the scale to translate that into what you might have to walk. Some compasses come with built-in rulers that figure the conversion automatically (more on that later).

Unfortunately, few trails or walkable paths in the woods are straight. You could try to estimate by measuring stretches that are almost straight and adding the results. One trick I learned from *Compass & Map Navigator* by Michael Hodgson (Globe Pequot, 2000), which I'm changing a bit due to inherent laziness, is to take a piece of solid copper wire and bend it so it follows the path you will take. Mark the ends, and then stretch out the wire and measure its length, getting a better approximation of the distance actually facing you, as in Figure 4-11.

By comparing the map to the landscape, you can orient the map and, by extension, yourself. That means you must still find your position and your direction. The former can come from careful observation, watching your surroundings, and matching the map position with what you see around you. You can also take coordinates (from a geocaching Web site or from your GPSr) and plot them directly on the map.

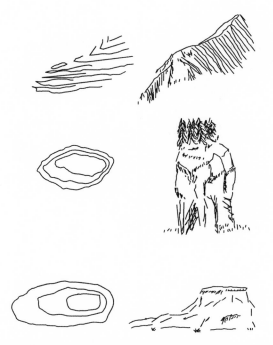

Figure 4-10 Topographic representations and corresponding geography

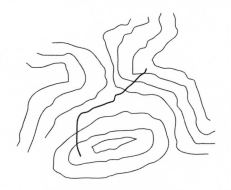

Trace your intended path
by bending wire along it.

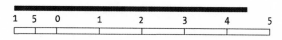

Straighten the wire and measure the
distance along the map scale.

Figure 4-11 Using wire as a ruler

Using the Map Grids

Grid coordinates are the lingua franca of the geographic world, and they are how you can place a cache location onto a map. You can transfer the numbers that indicate north/south and east/west and find the corresponding spot.

Maps usually have lines running vertically and horizontally, forming squares on the page. Sometimes there are tick marks on the map borders, and you must take a straightedge and draw lines connecting the respective pairs. Modern topographic maps will have tick marks or grids for both lat/lon and UTM.

Lat/Lon

With a lat/lon grid, any two adjacent latitude lines—or, for that matter, longitude lines—are separated by 2'30" on most topographic maps, as Figure 4-12 shows. Latitude increases from the bottom of the map to the top, and longitude increases from the right side to the left side.

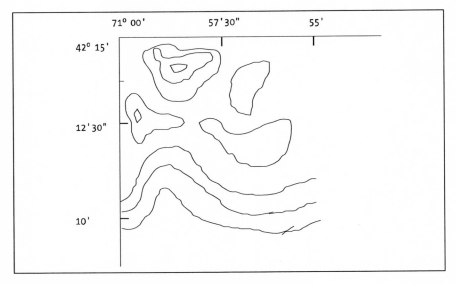

Figure 4-12 Example of latitude and longitude map grid

To place a point, look at its specified latitude and longitude coordinates and find the square on the map in which you would find the point. You know that the latitude of the point has to fall between the latitude lines that form the top and bottom of the square, and the longitude will be between the longitude lines that make the sides. (And if the point falls on one of the lines, it just makes things easier—carry on.)

You could try to estimate the point's location by guessing where the coordinates would fall. Or, to make life more exact, you could use a special ruler for measuring the distances in minutes and seconds. (The resources section has some sources for these rulers; just be sure that you buy one that matches the scale—1:24,000, 1:25,000, or 1:62,500—of your map.)

To place the point, first place the ruler's 0" mark on the lower latitude line. Orient the ruler so that the numbers go up towards north on the map, if the region is in the northern hemisphere. In the southern hemisphere, you have the ruler pointing south. Calculate how many minutes and seconds you must add to the lower latitude value to get your point's latitude. Draw a horizontal line at that point. (See Figure 4-13.)

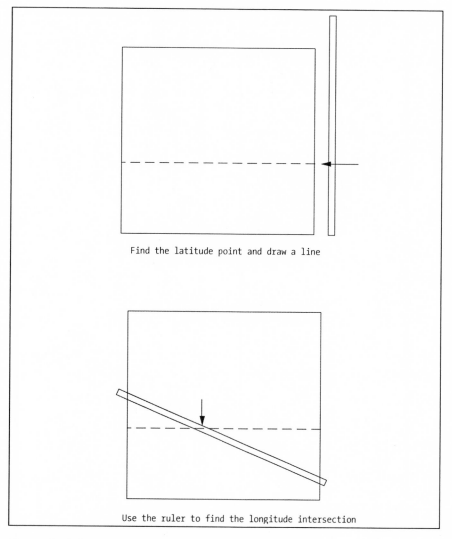

Find the latitude point and draw a line

Use the ruler to find the longitude intersection

Figure 4-13 Finding a location with lat/lon coordinates

Now you must determine how much to add to the lower-value longitude line (the right-most longitude) to get the longitude value at your point. Plotting the longitude is a little trickier because longitudes curve from pole to pole, so you have to get the correct angle. Put the ruler's 00" mark on the right-most longitude line and the 2'30" mark on the left-most longitude line. While keeping the ruler oriented this way, slide it up or down until the line you drew intersects the ruler at the number you calculated that you must add to the lower-value longitude line. That is your point, and X marks your cache.

Yes, it works. Yes, all the geocaching Web sites provide latitude and longitude coordinates, but they appear in decimal form, not minutes and seconds. This means you must convert your lat/lon value by using the example in Figure 4-14.

Start with the decimal degree.
183.745

Everything left of the decimal point is the whole degree.
183°

Multiply the remaining decimal part by 60.
.745 x 60 = 44.7

Everything left of the decimal point is the minutes.
44'

Multiply the remaining decimal part by 60.
.7 x 60 = 42

What remains are the seconds.
42"

Put everything together.
183° 44' 42"

Figure 4-14 Converting between degree decimals and minutes and seconds

One advantage of UTM is that you don't have to convert values at all, and plotting the coordinates is easier.

UTM

As with lat/lon, some maps have a full UTM grid, and others require you to take a straight edge and draw grid lines using border tick marks as guides. The values of the eastings increase west to east (left to right), and the northing values increase south to north (bottom to top). The difference between any two adjacent lines is 1,000 meters, or a kilometer.

To find a particular coordinate, you can take one of two approaches. To estimate the location, take the easting, find the two grid lines that are above and below its value, then find where it would more or less fall between the two. Do the same with the northing and find where lines passing through the two approximate values would intersect. (See Figure 4-15.)

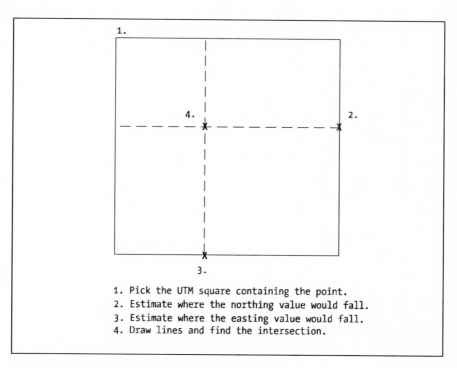

1. Pick the UTM square containing the point.
2. Estimate where the northing value would fall.
3. Estimate where the easting value would fall.
4. Draw lines and find the intersection.

Figure 4-15 Estimating a location by UTM coordinates

An easier approach is to use a UTM grid ruler, which is actually a set of squares that help you simultaneously determine the horizontal and vertical positions. Like the lat/lon ruler, you need a grid ruler that will match your map's scale. Typically, one UTM ruler will support multiple scales. Instead of a straight line, the UTM ruler offers a set of squares with grid marks. Calculate the differences between the left-hand easting line and desired easting coordinate, and between the bottom northing line and the northing coordinate. Now find the same values on the UTM ruler and place them on the easting and northing lines. The top right corner of the ruler's grid is the location you seek, as you can see in Figure 4-16.

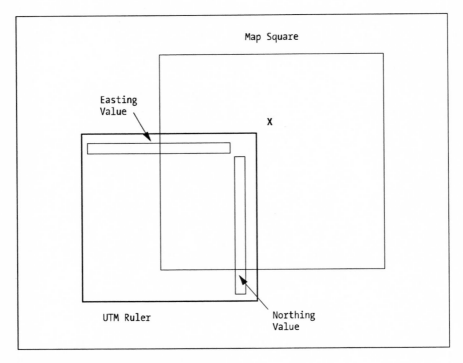

Figure 4-16 Using a UTM grid ruler

Don't underestimate the power of a map; there are some exceptionally good geocachers with at the time of this writing over one thousand finds to their credit who don't even own a GPSr. Instead, they pinpoint a cache's location on the map to within close of what a receiver could show, then start looking. However, a GPSr *can* make things easier.

Using a GPSr

Using a GPSr to know where you are (and where that cache is) does not take much time. However, you want the little time it takes to occur before you begin wandering about.

Setting a Waypoint

Every GPSr lets you set a waypoint. Usually, the approach is to set a man over-board (MOB) point and then to adjust the coordinates. The MOB terminology comes from boating; if someone falls overboard you want to immediately note where it happened so you can circle around and retrieve the person. A GPSr generally lets you press some button (exactly which one depends on the manu-facturer and model) that will record your location at that moment.

You could use this function to enter the waypoint of a cache location by marking any waypoint, then using the GPSr to change the coordinate values to those of your desired destination, but there's an easier approach: just down-load the cache coordinates to a computer, then send the coordinates from the computer to the GPSr. Geocaching.com supports a software package called EasyGPS (found at http://www.easygps.com), which stores the waypoints you've visited and the waypoints on your to-do list. The application is relatively easy to use and is free, although it does not support UTM coordinates. The company that makes it has a more powerful version, ExpertGPS, that does support UTM. It will let you draw routes on a map and download them to your GPSr, and it allows you to search for nearby features from a large database.

Where the MOB button becomes even more useful is right after you leave your car and start on foot. Always, always, always press it so you have the coor-dinates of your car, should you get lost on your search.

 NOTE This can be one of the toughest things to remember. I cannot even remember the number of times I have kicked myself on a trail for not setting my return point.

Goto

Now that you have the coordinates of your destination (in either lat/lon or UTM) and have stored your initial location so you can find your way back, you will want to use the goto feature. By specifying a waypoint, the GPSr can help you reach it by both showing the direction in which you need to travel and providing an estimate of the distance left to go.

Goto is a simple concept, but is potentially deceptive when you try to actually travel following the directions by using the bearing function.

Bearing

Knowing how far from you a waypoint is doesn't offer much help unless you know in what direction you need to travel. GPS units have a bearing function. An arrow or some other indicator points to the direction in which you must travel. If you start to turn in the wrong direction, the indicator shows that you must adjust your path.

However, I am wary of the bearing function. A GPSr is designed to find a single position, not determine direction. For the receiver to know how to reach a waypoint, it must know where you are traveling. That happens by the receiver taking a sampling of positions and using them to determine your direction and velocity. But this works well only if you are moving fast enough. At less than a couple of miles an hour, a receiver can lose track of how you are moving. So if you find yourself slowed by terrain, your orientation and the direction to the cache would go out the window—or out of the receiver's display. I've found myself pointed in exactly the opposite direction of the cache I sought. There are some potential solutions, like using the mapping function.

Mapping

With the mapping function, you can see the track of your movements, all in relation to the waypoint you seek. (See Figure 4-17 for an example.)

Figure 4-17 Example of a GPSr mapping function

Mapping works differently from the bearing function. Instead of acting like an electronic finger constantly pointing in the direction of a waypoint, mapping shows your movement in relationship to the waypoint. When you use mapping, the GPSr keeps a longer record of your positions, then draws a path connecting them, so you see a track of where you have been. At the same time, it shows the line of movement necessary to reach the waypoint along a straight line. Even when you slow down, your position relative to the cache remains. That allows you to move more slowly when you are nearing the hiding spot without running the risk of losing the direction. Now you might think that if the receiver could track that well in mapping, it could do so in bearing mode. But with the units I've used, it doesn't seem to. I don't argue; I just do what works.

Mapping can also help if you become lost. By looking at your tracks, you can see where you are and how you got there, which means you can find your way back. Figure 4-18 shows an example of my misadventures. I had been looking for a cache off-trail in some thick woods and, after finding it, got twisted about. I had foolishly not brought a map, so my compass showed a direction, but I didn't know what else was around me. But by checking the GPSr mapping, I noticed a fairly straight line that was from walking on a trail. Turning so that the mapping arrow pointed back to the trail, I moved back up the hill to a spot I remembered.

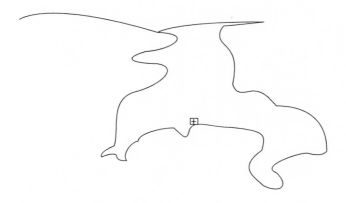

Figure 4-18 Using GPS mapping to get found

Handy for when you are lost or when you are looking for a cache is the scaling function. This allows you to zoom in and out of the map, which is helpful when you are nearing the cache and want to keep pointing the right way, or when you need to pull back for a broader view of the area.

Besides using mapping, you can also check the GPSr for the last bearing you had to the waypoint. You can then use a compass to continue walking along that bearing.

Compass

The compass must be one of the ten great inventions of history. To notice that certain metals are attracted by magnetism, then to build a device that associates the natural pull to the directions in a circle is something staggeringly brilliant. A baseplate or orienteering compass, as shown in Figure 4-19, can let you do marvels.

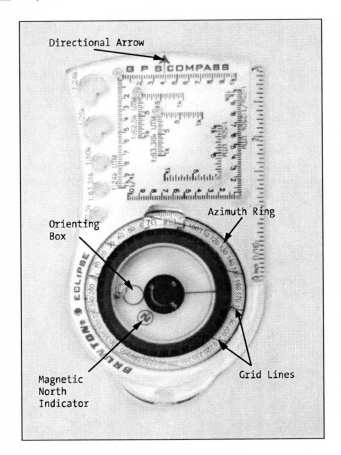

Figure 4-19 Example of a compass

Notice the various parts of the compass:

- Azimuth ring
- Directional arrow
- Magnetic north needle or indicator
- Orienting box
- Grid lines

The whole trick is that the needle keeps you oriented; it probably has a red side, pointing north, and a black side. The azimuth ring turns so that any direction on it can line up with the direction arrow. That directional arrow points in your direction of travel. Because the needle points north and the azimuth ring turns, you can specify any direction in relation to north by finding its bearing.

Bearings

Bearings offer a way of describing a direction, relative to north. Remember that any circle can be divided into 360 equally spaced degrees. If you stood on one spot and wanted to accurately describe your next direction, you could say, "I faced north, then turned clockwise X degrees." In other words, you have told someone to stand in a spot and rotate a certain amount, which will leave the person facing the direction in question. That turn, in degrees, is the bearing. (As I've been taken to task for sloppy terminology in the past by a surveyor, it is technically called an azimuth, but most backpackers and hikers use the words interchangeably.)

Conversely, the reverse direction, from that distant spot back to you, would be the back bearing. It is like the opposite point on a clock face that has 360 degrees rather than 12 hour positions. To get the back bearing of a bearing that is less than 180°, you add 180. If the bearing is greater than 180°, you subtract 180.

A compass provides a good way of measuring a bearing. When a compass comes from the factory, its orienting box points to north on the azimuth ring. If you turn the ring so that north points toward the fixed directional arrow, then turn the compass so that the red end of the needle is directly over the orienting arrow or box, then the directional arrow (and you) are pointed north.

To go along a particular bearing, you turn the ring so that the bearing number is at the top of the compass and in line with the directional arrow. Hold the compass horizontally (level) and turn your body so that the red end of the magnetic needle or indicator is over the orienting arrow or box, as shown in Figure 4-20.

The directional arrow now points in the direction of the specified bearing. Start walking. So long as you keep the magnetic needle above the orienting box, you continue to walk on that bearing.

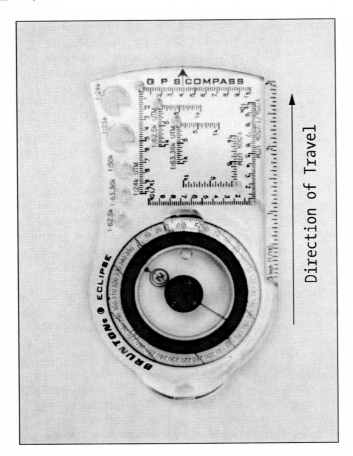

Figure 4-20 Walking along a bearing

What if you wanted to provide a bearing to someone? That is easy. Hold the compass horizontally and site along it in the direction for which you want a bearing. (You can look at some landmark in the distance to make this easier.) The red part of the needle, as always, points north. Turn the azimuth ring until the orienting arrow or box lines up with the red part of the needle or indicator, as Figure 4-21 shows.

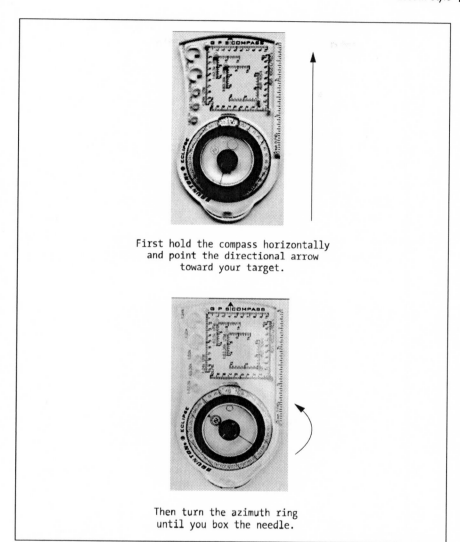

First hold the compass horizontally
and point the directional arrow
toward your target.

Then turn the azimuth ring
until you box the needle.

Figure 4-21 Shooting a bearing

The bearing you want will now be at the top of the compass.

Bearings and Maps

In general, though, you don't trade bearings with other people. Instead, you work between the real world and a map, so you must learn how to transfer bearings between the two. Here is how to take a bearing from the map and use it:

1. Find two points on the map: your current location (you can get that from your GPSr) and the one you wish to reach (presumably, the cache's location).

2. Put a corner of the bottom of the compass on your current location and swing that side of the base plate around until it lines up with your intended destination, as in Figure 4-22.

3. Turn the azimuth ring until its grid lines run parallel with those of the map and north on the ring points towards north on the map.

4. Read the bearing off the top of the compass.

Now you can follow the bearing using the previous directions.

To do the opposite and transfer a bearing from the world to the map, use the following steps:

1. Shoot a bearing with your compass.

2. Place the compass on your map.

3. Turn the entire compass (not just the azimuth ring) until its grid lines are parallel to those of the map and the ring's north points in the same direction as the map's.

4. While maintaining the compass's same orientation, slide the compass around until the bottom of one edge is on your location.

The edge of the compass and the directional arrow show the bearing. Now you can go back and forth between map and the land. There is just one little problem: north doesn't always mean north.

Magnetic Declination

Unfortunately, the magnetic north pole is not in the same spot as the geographic north pole. For most places on earth, there is a magnetic declination, which means at a given location, there is an angle between magnetic north and so-called true north, as Figure 4-23 shows. (For example, in Massachusetts, where I live, the magnetic declination is about 16 degrees west).

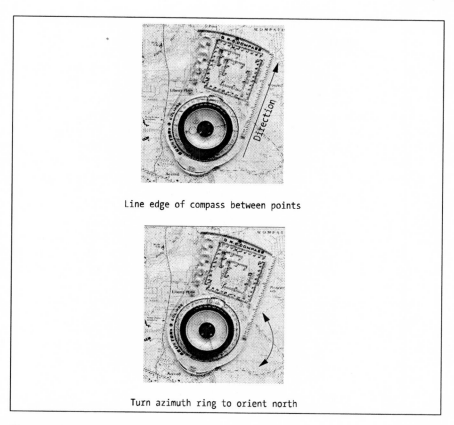

Line edge of compass between points

Turn azimuth ring to orient north

Figure 4-22 Taking a bearing from a map

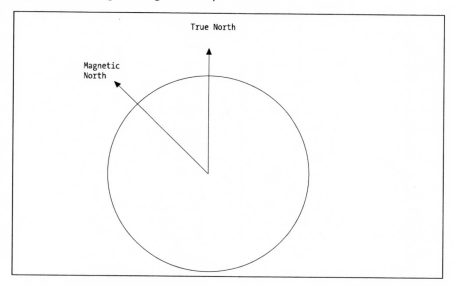

Figure 4-23 Magnetic declination

So when you set a compass to north and "box the needle" (rotate the orienting box or arrow so that it is directly below the red part of the magnetic needle), it actually points to magnetic north, not true north. This is fine, so long as everyone specifies that the bearings are taken with a magnetic north reference.

But many people specify bearings to true north, not magnetic north, mostly because maps are generally oriented to true north. In this case, you must correct for magnetic declination. That is why topographic maps generally have a declination notation on them. However, the magnetic north pole actually moves around, and magnetic north can change from year to year, altering declination. To be safe, you should check an appropriate reference (see the resources appendix) to find a region's current declination.

You can use simple arithmetic to adjust bearings for true north, but the rules are complicated. Depending on whether you are adjusting to bearings someone gives you, taking bearings off a map, or transferring bearings you've observed to a map, you sometimes add and sometimes subtract. Furthermore, the rules for eastern declination are exactly the opposite of those for western declination.

The adding and subtracting depend on whether you are trying to take a magnetic bearing in and of itself and adjust your reading to what it would be in true north, or if you are working back and forth between compass and map. That is because the circumstances determine whether your bearing has been taken east or west of your reference (magnetic or true north), and that depends completely on what you are doing.

Let's start with western declination, where magnetic north seems to lie west of true north. (That is, an unadjusted compass pointing "north" is actually pointing to a spot that is west of true north.)

Say you take a bearing and want to transfer that bearing to a map with a true north grid. (Again, you have not adjusted the compass at all.) Then you must *subtract* the declination value from your bearing to the true north bearing that will be correct on the map. That is because your original reference (magnetic north) is west of your final reference (true north), and you have to remove that distance to have a bearing that will work with the map.

If you measure a bearing on a map that has a true north grid and want to transfer it to your unadjusted compass in the face of a western declination, you must *add* the declination to your bearing from the map, because your original reference (true north) is east of your final reference (magnetic north), and you have to make up the difference to have a bearing that will work with the unadjusted compass, as you see in Figure 4-24.

Similarly, say you want to take a bearing on an unadjusted compass and transfer it to a true north grid. In this case, though, the declination is east. Now your original reference point (magnetic north) is east of your final reference point (true north), and you have to *add* the declination amount to the bearing to have something that will correctly work with the map.

And if you have an eastern declination and are going from the map to the unadjusted compass, your original reference is true north, your final reference, magnetic north, lies east of it, and you have to *subtract* the declination from the bearing.

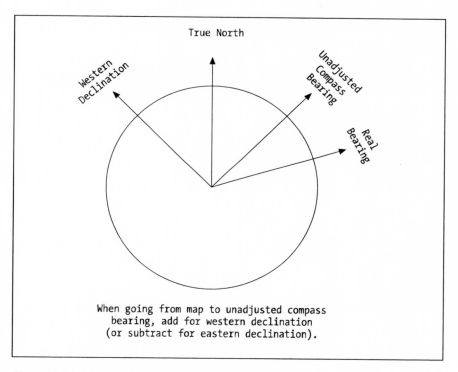

Figure 4-24 Adjusting for declination from map bearing

This can be difficult to keep straight on plenty of sleep and a full stomach, parked in a recliner, listening to calming music from the eighteenth century. Go out in the cold with dusk around the corner and food only a faint promise, and you have the makings of a headache with the nearest aspirin unfathomably far away. Skip all the arithmetic nonsense and just buy a compass with a declination adjustment. Then you don't have to make any adjustments, and all your bearings will be given off true north, totally eliminating the problem.

All that you will have to monitor is your placement of the compass on the map. After you adjust the declination, the orienting box no longer lines up with north on the azimuth ring, as Figure 4-25 shows.

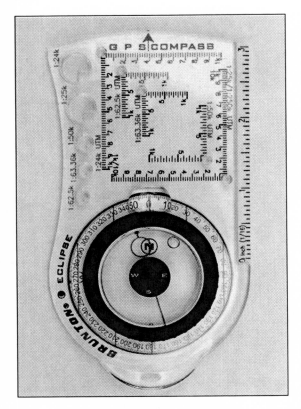

Figure 4-25 Compass alignment after declination adjustment

When you turn the azimuth ring to orient to north on the map, the ring's grid lines will be parallel to those of the map. North on the ring will point north. It's just that the orienting arrow will point off at an angle. It is the price you pay for not needing to tote a calculator.

There is a difference between true north and grid north, but this is usually so small (well under a degree) as to be cavalierly tossed aside. Sticklers for accuracy beyond need can adapt the previous description of how to handle differences between references and be right, right, right. I'll simply enjoy a beer while they struggle with their woods-bound arithmetic.

There is another type of unexpected type of declination. Because compasses work on magnetism, large pieces of metal can disrupt their operation. This can include vehicles, buildings, flag poles, and your Uncle Henry's cranial plate. For an example, take your compass into a car and then watch the needle as you move it close to the front windshield then back again. Chances are you will see the needle swing. Some large rocks will even affect the reading, so look about you before trusting what the compass says.

Orienting the Map

It can be difficult sometimes to see how a topographic map corresponds to the land around you. In such times, you can use the compass to orient it and make the correspondence easier to see:

1. Turn the azimuth ring so that north lines up with the directional arrow of the compass.

2. Hold the map horizontally.

3. Turn the entire compass so that the grid lines on the map and the compass are parallel, and north on the azimuth ring points to north on the map.

4. Turn the entire map until the compass arrow is directly over the orienting box.

Now the map is pointing to true north (assuming that you have declination set) and everything is oriented. But sometimes with the best of efforts, you will find yourself wondering exactly where you are. This is when triangulation can play a key role.

Triangulation

Remember how a GPSr uses triangulation to discover its location? You can do the same with a compass and map by using these steps:

1. Orient the map to the land.

2. Find two landmarks around you.

3. Find them on the map.

4. Shoot a bearing to one landmark.

5. Draw a line using the back bearing from the landmark on the map.

6. Shoot a bearing to the other landmark.

7. Draw a line using the back bearing from that landmark.

Where the two lines intersect on the map is your position. (See Figure 4-26.)

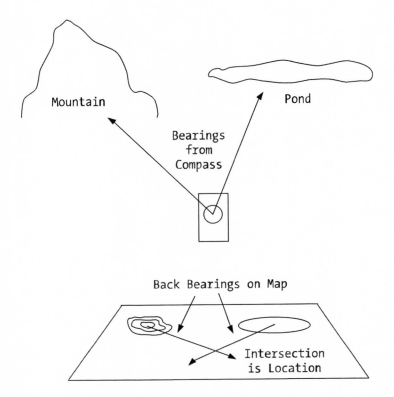

Mountain

Pond

Bearings
from
Compass

Back Bearings on Map

Intersection
is Location

Figure 4-26 Triangulation

That, however, is still an approximate position, because shooting bearings and transferring them to a map is inexact. If you shot three bearings, instead of intersecting in a point, they would form a triangle, and your position would be somewhere within it.

Altimeter

A topographic map shows heights for more than the amusement of readers and the profit of map makers. Altitude can help pinpoint your location. For example, you might take a bearing off a landmark and plot the back bearing on a map. The resulting line might intersect the trail you are on in three different places. (See Figure 4-27.)

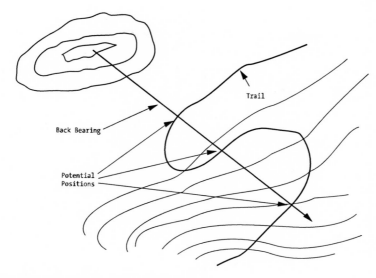

Figure 4-27 Using altitude to establish position

However, you may not need to take a second bearing if the three points of the trail have three different altitudes. An altimeter will eliminate two possibilities, leaving the one which is your position.

You can also use height in other ways, like observing slopes and their directions or using it to help note where you leave a trail. But nothing is as ultimately useful as common sense, and the best tool you have lies between your ears.

Using Your Brain

Being lost may mean having an uncertain position, but it also means being absent-minded or distracted. When you don't want to be lost, you want the opposite mental state: attentive and alert.

Getting a Real Reading

A GPSr will show altitude, but it's incredibly inaccurate and not something to be trusted. Using its height reading could have you confidently marching into the nearest tar pit. Either keep a separate altimeter, or find a GPSr that has a separate altimeter function. And remember that your altimeter needs to be calibrated each day, so you either have to set it at sea level or calibrate it to a known height, like an identified point on a topographic map. f you are out overnight, make a note of the reading at your camp site and recalibrate in the morning to that height. If you are out overnight, make a note of the reading at your camp site and recalibrate in the morning to that height.

The easiest way to avoid being lost is to keep finding yourself as you travel. Losing your way usually happens through inattention. For example, people will go bounding down trails without a thought of how they will return. And yet, turning around every now and again can work a world of wonders. Suddenly, that stretch of path ahead as you return begins to look familiar.

Trail marks are not enough to rely on. There is one state park relatively near me that has an extensive set of marked trails. Yet the placards that number the intersections face in only one direction, and you must turn around to see them from the other. In another park, multiple trails have the same reflective white cards as blazes, which makes telling one from the other difficult.

Navigation tools can be flawed. Reflected signals can cause a GPSr to provide faulty information, particularly deep in the woods or near large rocks or even buildings. (Check Chapter 3, "The Technology.") You might misapply arithmetic and calculate the wrong back bearing from a compass. The barometric pressure might have changed, throwing your altimeter out of calibration. Even maps can be poorly drawn and misleading. Always compare results with those of other tools and with your own observation, and challenge your own deductions, too.

If you do find yourself lost, backtrack to the last point at which you knew where you were and start over, taking more care. And practice using all your tools before you must depend on them. Go to a large field with your compass, face north, mark your location with a stick or a coin, then set a 90° bearing and walk it, watching the compass while not looking up. Take 25 paces, then change to 180° and walk 25 paces more. Turn to 270° and go another 25 paces, only to turn back to 360° (or 0°, the same bearing by a different name) and go another 25. You should be close to the spot you marked. Set a waypoint on your GPS, then go across the field and use goto to seek that spot. See how the device works at different speeds, in different orientations. How parallel to the ground do you need to keep the GPSr to keep receiving the satellite signals?

Once you have this practice under your belt, consider the next chapter on preparing for your hike.

GPSr (In)accuracy

This exercise will teach you an important lesson: how accuracy can suffer even from one minute to the next. Kelly Markwell, a geocacher from the Chicago area who is technical editor for this book, tried something like this when he took his first receiver out of the box. "I set a waypoint at the mailbox, walked halfway down the block and hit GOTO," he says, instructing the device to direct him back to his mailbox. "When I came back I was about 25 feet from the mailbox when it said 2.94 feet away. I learned that for geocaching, I needed to widen my search radius from 'right here' to 'somewhere around here.'" Ultimately, technology is only a tool and not a substitute for effort.

5

A Good Walk

"Walking is man's best medicine."—Hippocrates

It all falls into a rhythm: arm swings conducting, the slow drumming of soles on dirt punctuated by the soft sway of a day pack, the sweep of clothing against itself, the emphatic spatter of snow from a low-hanging branch.

Even at its simplest level, geocaching requires hiking—even more than it requires a GPSr. Although it is possible to seek caches without using a receiver, you can't sit about and wait for caches to travel to you. So to geo-cache, you need knowledge of hiking at least as much as you need knowledge of technology.

The challenge posed by the hiking or walking varies with the terrain and difficulty of the cache. A long hike on mountainous terrain will obviously call for more effort than a stroll along a manicured path in a city park. No matter which you favor, though, the more you know about being outdoors, the better. You can be caught by unexpected conditions in either, find poison ivy in either, become sunburned or chilled in either, or kick yourself for forgetting the one item that would have been handy in either.

Although you will experience the occasional mistake, some practice will smooth out many potential rough spots in your outdoor experience. It may be that you are an experienced hiker and even backpacker, in which case most of the following information you will know; even so, do check the section on what to put in your pack, because some items are of particular interest to the geo-cacher. If you haven't gone on extended strolls in a while, then this chapter should be helpful.

Day hiking is fine for easier caches, but there are some that require extended effort, and sometimes an overnight stay. Backpacking is beyond the scope of this book—it requires a volume or more in its own right. Fortunately, there are a number of fine books on the subject: informative, illustrative, and packed with writing worth reading just for its own pleasure. Appendix A lists some that I've particularly enjoyed.

Getting Ready

No matter how long or short your journey, you need to prepare yourself. The most important step is planning. Proper planning means considering a number of things:

- Knowing your route

- Knowing your limits

- Planning for problems

- Having what you need

Like many people, I have looked up a cache and immediately taken off to find it on a whim, having checked no map, no local authority, not even a weather forecast. But consider that when you go someplace nearby that is familiar, effectively you are applying planning. Even if you don't know a specific spot, you know the area's general terrain. You are familiar with the local weather patterns. It's planning based on information you have collected over a long period of time.

When you begin to consider caches farther away, however, planning should become more formal. As the distance and unfamiliarity increase, so does your preparation to answer important questions. What will the terrain be like, and what route will you take? How should you dress for the temperatures you might expect? Will there be a problem with biting insects, like the vicious greenhead flies found in many parts of the eastern United States at all the most inconvenient times? What range of weather can you expect? Are you looking for a difficult cache that requires equipment or training, such as scuba or technical rock climbing? As things become more challenging, you can go beyond having a plan by preparing yourself. Work your way up to the level of activity and exertion that you will experience.

> **NOTE** I am far from a svelte and athletic man. Yet I'm capable of vigorous hiking up reasonably hilly terrain because I prepared over time. I began regular walking and hiking, first for 20 minutes at a time. Now I regularly clear out of the house, clearing my head at the same time, for an hour or more, covering between three and four miles, uphill and down. Trust me: if I can do this, so can you. In warmer weather, I trade off between walking and cycling, adding some variety and keeping things from getting stale. Sometimes I even turn exercise into an outing by cycling a few miles to a coffee house and knocking back a drink before returning.

Whatever you do, do it on actual roads and trails. I tried using a fitness center, but inevitably found that all the preparation time on a treadmill would still quickly leave me huffing. My theory is that because treadmills move the surface under you, and don't force you to fight road resistance, the only real exercise you get is in lifting your legs up and down. No mark against it, but I've found it to do little in building stamina for actual travel.

Before going off on any caching adventure, you should know that it will be within your limits. Attempting more extreme variations of geocaching—like underwater searches that approach the limits of recreational scuba—without proper preparation and instruction is a fast way to the nearest morgue. Short of that, though, you still want to make an evaluation. If you are just beginning to walk regularly, don't plan on a steep, long hike that will leave you gasping.

Being prepared extends beyond you to include everyone and everything that you might have in tow. Some cache locations are potentially unsafe for young children (cache page descriptions generally mention this). The gear you will use can also have an effect; no matter your state of fitness, expecting to complete a long hike in new boots that have yet to see adequate break-in time is asking for trouble.

Even when you don't ask for trouble, some often appears. There might be a problem at the location. You might find that you have spent considerable time without finding the cache. It doesn't matter; things do go wrong, which is why you need a contingency plan. If you are in a local park, that might be as simple as packing it in to return another day. If out on an overnight hike, you should leave your route and expected return or contact time with someone who can call the authorities should you seemingly disappear. And if you are fine in such a case, you make hell-and-high-water sure that you call when expected. There is never an excuse for letting people worry and hit the panic button because of your sloppiness.

Wherever you go, you will need some basic things: clothing, navigation aids, water, snacks, and spare batteries (some geocachers nickname them "GPS food"), among other things. Because you can't count on the local geo-convenience store, you have to bring these things with you.

Suiting Up

The most important thing you might bring, if for no other reason than to mollify the authorities, is clothing. The most universal place to start is at the bottom.

Feet

Picking footgear used to be relatively easy because the market offered relatively few choices. You could buy full mountaineering boots, midweight versions, or sneakers. Today the choice is limited only by the size of the display case. Figure 5-1 shows some of the possibilities.

Figure 5-1 Some choices of hiking footwear
Photo courtesy of Vasque. Copyright 2004 Vasque. All Rights Reserved.

The wide variety of footgear falls into several discrete categories:

- Mountaineering boots: These offer a foundation for the most demanding mountain climbing. They are great for going up tremendously difficult landscapes while carrying large loads and wondering if your life insurance is paid up. They are heavy and totally unnecessary for geocaching, unless some cacher has been sneaking up into the Alps.

- Heavyweight boots: When you are out for an extended stint of backpacking and are on reasonably punishing ground with heavy loads (one-third or more of your theoretic body weight), your feet will thank you for this support. But if not out on a serious trek, their weight on your feet can be a drag.

- Midweight boots: This is the start of potential footwear choices for most general hiking and, as an extension, geocaching. At 3.5 to 5 pounds a pair, you will not forget that you are wearing them. But if you are on hilly ground or have your own heft, like me, they offer support that can make the difference between fun and fuming.

- Lightweight boots: Over the last ten years or so, companies have been combining synthetic materials with the occasional leather swatch to create boots that approach a shoe's lightness, yet still manage to offer the support an average-sized person might need to bear a pack for a few days in the woods.

- Trail shoes: Not out for an overnight stay? Then these might do the trick. Offering more support than street shoes, they are lighter and less expensive than boots and made for the majority of trails you will find in parks and forests.

- Sandals: Some companies make special sandals for hiking on trails, or for switching from boots when you've pitched the tent and want to cool your feet.

- Athletic shoes: Call them sneakers, running shoes, or cross-trainers, they are comparable to, and probably even lighter than, trail shoes. Some people swear by them for geocaching.

It would seem that the best way to choose footgear would be to logically deduce what your particular needs are. Even after considering such things as your size, how much baggage you will carry to the trail, and what the footing will be, people have remarkably less choice in the matter than they think, no matter how well-stocked the local outdoor store might be.

To paraphrase the Harry Potter books, it's the boots that choose the hiker. I've worn fancy Italian-made hiking boots that lasted for many years, and found them less comfortable and more expensive than what I use now, which is a midweight store brand from EMS. However, I know people who swear by Gore-Tex lightweights, or even by an old pair of sneakers, and if you are sticking to easy trails, that might be fine. Here's a good rule of thumb: the more weight you will carry (whether in a pack or, like myself, on your person) or the rougher the terrain, the sturdier your footwear must be.

After fit, brand and features come second and third, in my opinion. If the boot gives you about a half-inch of room in front of your toes, barely lets you slip an index finger between it and your heel, and doesn't let your foot careen forward when used on a 20° slope, buy it. You can make minor modifications, such as using sole inserts or getting the seller to stretch out a point on the leather, but keep the emphasis on *minor*; if the boot isn't a good fit to start, a different pair of socks isn't going to fix it.

That brings us to actually buying the boot. You can find Web sites dedicated to helping the person heading to a trail save money. It is easy on the wallet, and the variety can be overwhelming, but my strong suggestion is don't buy your boots online. Too many things that can go wrong when sizing your feet; I've yet to see a catalog or monitor provide a Brannock Device, one of those gadgets used in shoe stores to measure the length and width of feet. And fit doesn't stop there. If you buy your footwear from a reputable big chain (EMS or REI, for example) or go to a specialty shop, you should be able to try the boots or shoes indoors for a time until you have a sense that they will work for you. If they don't ultimately fit, you bring them back and find something else.

> **NOTE** Sometimes the stores are more generous than might seem reasonable. I talked with an outdoor consultant and Outward Bound leader who had purchased a pair of heavy-duty mountaineering boots, dropping a pretty penny for them. She used them periodically (only on major climbs) for two years, always waiting for the boots to finally break in and loosen a bit. It never happened, so she brought the boots back—and the shop actually took the return!

The one departure you can take from making your own personal in-store appearance is when you already know that a particular brand and model are like angel's wings caressing your feet. If you need a replacement pair and the exact thing you want is on a Web site for a little less, buy it online and save the money.

Be sure to wear the socks you plan to use with the boots or shoes before trying them on. For hiking boots, years ago this would have meant at least two pairs: a rough wool outer, and an inner either of silk or polypropylene that would let moisture from the foot pass through. Many experienced backpackers still recommend the dual approach. I've recently been trying some Merino wool socks, though, that have an almost fleece-like interior. The result is good wicking of sweat, reliable warmth, and exceptional comfort. You could go with one of the major brands, like SmartWool, but I've found that some of the chains will have quality alternatives that are less expensive. Again, at the local EMS, I found some that have been working earnestly for the last couple of years, running only half the price of the more prestigious names.

No matter what sort of sock appeals to you, your footwear probably still needs time for breaking in, and the heavier the boot, the more time you will need. I don't care what some advertising "genius" promises: if you immediately go on a serious hike with new boots or shoes—no matter how light and flexible—without a breaking-in period, you run the risk of breaking in your feet instead. Ignore that fact, and you run the risk of developing blisters. As boots get heavier, they are stiffer and take even longer to work with your foot. How to put this delicately? Ah, yes: Get the damn boots before you head on a serious outing, and leave yourself time enough to break them in adequately. Limping about and wincing are fine for courting sympathy, but are of little practical use when geocaching.

NOTE Kelly Markwell told me of having bought midweight hiking boots the day before hiking two miles for a cache. He had no problems, and the pair still serves him well. It's great if things work out well, but I can remember being in London, picking up a pair of lightweight walking shoes, taking them out for the day over many miles, and bringing a pair of sore feet back to the hotel room. You might get away with it, but is the lack of planning worth the potential pain and inconvenience?

There are a number of techniques for breaking in footwear, including lacing them up and wearing them out in the rain. The wet can soften the leather and help it mold to your foot faster. Such extremes seem so. . . extreme. My own preference is to wear the boots once on a moderately short walk and notice if any spots on my foot are feeling pressure, evidenced by either irritation or reddening of the skin. If so, the next time I try on the boot, it's with some preventative care in the form of moleskin or molefoam, products meant to cushion blisters. I place sections strategically around the bad spot on my foot. Given a couple of weeks of a half-hour a day or less, I found my current boots gave in and stopped irritating. If you are having an unusual amount of trouble with a pair, see the store.

After a few uses, when it's become painlessly (hopefully) obvious that the gear has become part of your ensemble, consider some waterproofing. Check the manufacturer's literature and ask the store what type would work well with your shoes or boots, because some will need wax- or silicone-based treatment, and others demand oil. There are products for treating the seams, and it's sensible to take care of those potential leaks before treating the rest of the boot. No sense in making it impossible for the substance to find its way to the seams through the barrier the more general waterproofing will offer.

Boots or shoes with the proper socks are great in fair weather, but you can't always count on that for hiking—or geocaching. When things get wet, so can the inside of boots. Gaiters make a comforting friend at such times. Gaiters are treated pieces of cloth that wrap around your lower leg and fasten to the top and underneath a boot. Although there are short models, gaiters that rise up the calf, like the ones in Figure 5-2, will keep snow from sneaking down the collar of your footwear, and can even let you wade short distances in a stream while staying high and dry. Gaiters are even good in dry conditions, because they can keep dirt and pebbles and other trail schmootz from sneaking between boot and ankle.

When it comes to ice, you may need additional help. Slipping your way about is never pleasant and is a good way to land in a cast. Anyone climbing glaciers generally uses crampons, clamping affairs that add spikes to the bottom of your boots, giving every step additional bite. For the average trail, however—especially those used by most cachers to hide their stuff—using crampons is like swatting a mosquito with a sledge hammer.

Figure 5-2 Gaiters
Photo courtesy of Outdoor Research.

I've been using a crampon substitute called YakTrax. Instead of employing spikes that will seriously damage indoor flooring, each YakTrax is a large rubber band sporting a lattice of long, thin springs. Their grip on a slippery surface, even an iced-over wooden deck, is excellent. Testing them against a boot or shoe alone, I found myself able to walk reasonably well instead of gingerly stepping to avoid suddenly landing in a sitting position. Their one drawback is that they can occasionally slip off, so you must make periodic checks of their faithfulness. YakTrax makes a professional model that seems as though it would strap on more reliably, though I haven't gotten my hands on it—or my feet in it.

When ice is less of a problem but drifts of white powder abound, think of snowshoes. You may envision the traditional webbed wooden frames that look like tennis racquets. While those are still available, the long-standing trend is now for metal frames that use a tough plastic decking, like the ones in Figure 5-3.

Learning to use them is relatively easy (at least I thought so until a friend told me about her experience of trying them, stepping on one with the other, and toppling herself into the nearest snow bank). Small crampons at the toe help dig into packed terrain. Traversing slopes, or heading uphill or down, involves driving the snowshoe's edge, toe, or heel into the snow to gain purchase. Most snowshoes let you use almost any type of boot, so you can skip specialized footwear. Some brands to look for are Redwing, Atlas, and Tubbs.

Figure 5-3 Snowshoe
Photo courtesy Tubbs Snowshoe Co., Stowe, VT.

Backpackers have also traditionally used Nordic skis to travel cross-country. For geocaching, though, they are less useful, unless you are primarily interested in covering a lot of ground to reach the caching location. Skis are too clumsy for the omnidirectional shifting you must do while seeking.

Body

The rest of you also needs appropriate covering, and the different elements have different requirements, but there are some common threads. Whatever the weather, you want sweat to pass easily from your body. Cotton might sound great, and a comfortable t-shirt and pair of jeans are suitable for a moderate, dry day. When the weather gets extreme, though, cotton poses problems.

Cotton is a poor material for wicking sweat. Instead, cotton traps the water, effectively becoming a liquid sheet bound by a matrix of threads. When you are active, the shirt gets wet and stays wet. In hot weather, that will keep your body from cooling. In cold weather (you might be amazed at how much you can perspire when snow is on the ground), cotton is like wearing a refrigerator, because water transmits heat about 20 times more efficiently than air, effectively pulling heat from your body when you need it most

Good alternatives to cotton are plentiful. Wool is strong and traps far less water than cotton, which is why it's such a good component of hiking socks. Silk can be good, but really expensive. Consider instead the advice Dustin Hoffman's character in *The Graduate* received: plastics. Specially designed polyester-based fabrics do a fantastic job of keeping your skin dry and wicking moisture outward. Although generally a die-hard natural fibers fan, I've become a convert over the last few years. Even the polyester underwear designed for active use beats cotton all hollow; I've found that it is less prone to causing rashes because no wet material rubs your skin.

In summer, I tend to favor a short-sleeved t-shirt (sometimes cotton, because I hate wasting my existing ensemble from various high-tech corporate giveaways) and light warm-up trousers. Yes, many people like shorts, but if I'm going to be off trail at all and coming in contact with plants, I want to avoid poison ivy, poison oak, and poison sumac. I can always wear a pair of gym shorts underneath, giving me the option of dropping the extra protection when I'm both safe and overheated.

When the rain comes, it's necessary to avoid cotton if you will be outside for long, especially because the temperature could drop a score of degrees almost immediately, depending on your location. Although I do have a full raincoat, the typically gentle drops of the Northeast allow me to rely on a jacket of Gore-Tex, a name-brand coated nylon that does a fair job of repelling the wet while providing some breathability. However, remember that Gore-Tex, like all the other similar products, can lose its integrity and capability by being scratched and abraded by rocks, briars, trees, or other outdoor sources of scouring. You can get sprays from outdoor shops to recoat the fabric, though over the last two years, mine has worked fine. If you are in an area prone to heavy rain, a full raincoat may be become your first choice, along with rain pants.

In winter, the sensible approach is to layer clothing. I move to a long-sleeved T-shirt—always polyester, as my attempts at using cotton jerseys left me shivering under my coat. I know that many people opt for polyester long underwear, but I find that even when the temperature drops to the mid-20s Fahrenheit (sub-zero Celsius), I get too hot. It's easier to start off being a little cold and quickly warm up than it is to carry the extra weight of layers that will only have to come off—with no guarantee of personal modesty while changing. For trousers, I've been using some from Pacific Trails. They look like warm-up bottoms, but have Teflon-treated ripstop nylon with an inner lining similar to the Norwegian net t-shirts, beloved by many backpackers, that traps an additional layer of air between the outer shell and your skin. There is a dearth of pockets, except for one used to actually turn the garment inside out and stuff it into a self-contained pouch for easy storage in a pack. Unfortunately, a recent glance at the company's Web site showed not a sign, reinforcing my suspicion that proven utility is the death knell for fashion.

Trousers and a t-shirt will leave you cold when the mercury is down, which is why you need a coat. Collective experience says you should grab the fluffiest down sheath you can find and revel in its warmth. That certainly works, except for a few major problems. One is that wet down is about as cold and miserable as wet skin. Another is the binary property of a down coat: it is either on or off. That ignores the many situations in geocaching in which you'll find yourself too hot sealed up and too cold with a jacket over the shoulder.

Opt for an alternative to down. I came across a two-part coat at EMS— the Gore-Tex shell I mentioned before (lots of pockets, to make up for the trousers), and a choice of zip-in linings. I have a couple of compatible PolarFleece jackets, which are warm even when damp. I can use either fleece in combination with the shell, or use one on its own. If I need a bit of extra warmth on a cool day—more than a t-shirt but less than a full jacket—a warm vest can be just the perfect choice, and it stows conveniently in a backpack.

To avoid becoming a human hot house, I like the traditional approach of zippers, and not just on the front. Adding some in the arm pits lets you open up and vent heat and moisture. If you become chilled (it's easy to forget that you unzipped them yesterday), a simple tug will bring warmth. Both my shell and liner have pit zips, which can be awkward to manage, especially with a pack, but it's worth the minor inconvenience.

Head and Hands

You lose a honking huge amount of heat through your head: 40 percent or more. In the winter, this can mean the difference between comfort and serious problems with the cold. That is why you always must carry a hat; yes, your mother was right, especially if you are as follicly challenged as I.

There are high- and low-tech solutions to cover your cranium. I've tried many in the past, from wool knits (too scratchy) to generic polyester (don't like the feel). Last year, I gave PolarFleece a try with good results, and that's what I now favor. In moderate weather, I like a lined Irish wool cap, though with enough hair you might need nothing. In hot weather, I find some covering necessary to avoid a top-side sunburn. In that situation, I've experimented with one thing and the next before settling on a Tilley-style hat. The brim is broad enough to shade the face some, and the material, a light cotton (a good use of the fabric) sits easily. Figure 5-4 shows some of the toppers that have topped my list.

Figure 5-4 Some practical hats
Photo courtesy of Outdoor Research.

However, the best hat is one you wear when you need to. If a style is uncomfortable or inadequate, for land's sake don't do as I say, but do as I do, and try a few things until something works for you. This will change with conditions, too. My local weather is moderated by coastal conditions. But there are many places and times in which a full balaclava, with a pull-down face mask, is a wise choice.

All hats will get too warm at times, whether in summer or winter. In such cases, doff, doff, doff. You can always replace the hat. One advantage of a soft cotton hat in summer is that you can soak it in water and put it back on your head for no-fuss air-conditioning. I learned this trick from my scuba instructor on a blistering August morning in a part of Massachusetts where you need a heavy wet suit even in summer. This meant a hot walk to and from the car, dressed head-to-foot in rubber. When emerging from the water, I could pull the hood off my face and don the wet hat to make the trek more bearable.

Hands can also succumb to cold and numbness, though they seem more impervious in the heat. You can find insulated gloves, mittens, glove or mitten shells to fit over insulated liners, and a whole list of things that could set you back $100 to $200. For my typical geocaching needs, I have found that a pair of rag wool mittens lined with Thinsulate (warm and lightweight insulation material) can be good. Although they don't allow the dexterity of gloves, there is enough flexibility to operate the buttons on my GPSr. In very cold weather, I do think about using mitten shells to cut the wind. Again, though, whatever works for you is a good choice.

Other Gear

With your clothing, boots, and GPSr (as well as compass and map), what else could you possibly need? Well, plenty. Maybe. Let's start with things that will help you get around.

Walking Aids

There are times when unadorned boots need the help of gaiters and even crampons. Other accessories can be useful, too. I remember reading years ago in an earlier version of *The Complete Walker* about Colin Fletcher's affaire d'amour with a walking stick. His original was a sturdy bamboo staff, since replaced by a succession of other approaches when the first simply wore out.

Although his advice on everything else seemed sound, I dismissed the idea of carrying a walking stick, until recently. Maybe it is age, or possibly the willingness to toss to the winds the whole back-and-forth of why do I need it. (A staff looks cool; no, I will resemble nothing more than the hind quarters of a donkey.) So I picked up a likely candidate in some woods a few miles from my home, shaved off the bark, and started using it. Wonder of wonders, it's a pleasure to carry. When footing is slick, even when using my YakTrax, I plant the stick and steady myself. There is also the primordial cadence of a stick thumping the ground, a tempo that has been around for thousands of years. It is reassuring, as if reminding your body that some things really do not change. The right side of Figure 5-5 shows an example of a higher tech walking staff.

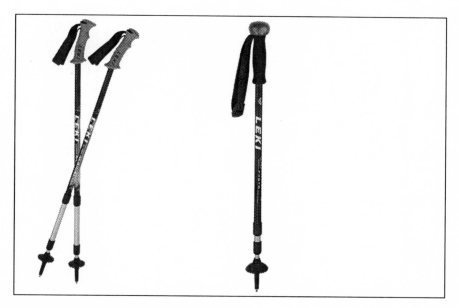

Figure 5-5 Trekking poles and a walking staff
Photo courtesy of LEKI USA.

If you want to interject a note of style and fancy in a staff, consider a diamond willow walking stick. This wood gets buried in snow for long stretches of time every year and, for reasons that seem to be up for some debate, has a number of diamond-shaped indentations with interesting coloring. When sanded to show contrasting patterns between heartwood and sapwood, the effect is a stick that runs from clean white to fertile red. I purchased a finished stick on eBay for $20, and another three blanks, ready for carving, for $25.

Tradition is great, but the latest trend is trekking poles. They are something like ski poles that you use while walking. In theory, weight is taken off your back, feet, and especially knees and put onto your arms. While on the trail, you can adjust their lengths not only to suit your particular height, but also to suit particular terrain. Walking across a steep incline, for example, you can lengthen the downhill pole and shorten the uphill so you can continue moving in a normal manner without stretching your arms uncomfortably to accommodate the uneven terrain. I've never tried trekking poles, but Karen Berger, a colleague and outdoor writer who has completed more long distance backpacking than I can mentally contemplate, says "I can't say enough good about them." She doubts that she would have successfully completed the Appalachian Trail (yes, Georgia to Maine) without the assistance of a pair. The left side of Figure 5-5 shows a pair. Having a pair of poles is also a shortcut should you ever need to improvise a shelter, as Figure 5-6 shows, whether the temperature is warm, or you need emergency protection in the snow.

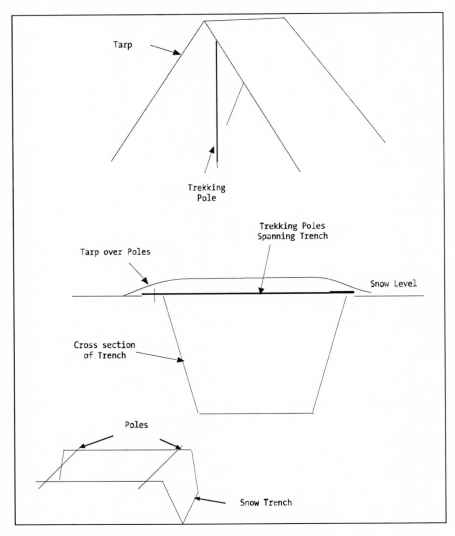

Figure 5-6 Improvising shelter with trekking poles and a tarp

Hopefully, you will not find yourself in need of living off (or in) the land. Nevertheless, there's more equipment that can offer a wealth of occasional benefits *if* you bring it with you.

Navigation Paraphernalia

You will want enough tools for navigation. This means the compass and the map, which you should either have waterproofed or placed in a case, as suggested in Chapter 3.

Certainly the GPS unit counts. When not in use (like when you are virtually on top of the cache location), you can stow it in a pocket or pack. Some models have available cases that can hang from a belt, like a cell phone, but I don't see that as necessary.

Navigation is hard if you cannot see. If you know you won't be out late, that might not be a problem, but consider a few points. If you start late, it is easy to get caught with the light running out just when you would like it. Also, if you are on the east side of a mountain, or submerged in woods, or even in a valley with the wrong exposure, you could see your light cut faster than you expected.

Barring the negative, accentuate the positive for a moment. Many cachers love the thrill of chasing through the woods at night, only artificial light keeping them on the path and the hunt. I also find hiking at night a pleasure, even though friends and family are often sure that I'm going to be ingested by some mutant coyote that was raised too near a nuclear power plant. At times, when the moon is out and the stars are shining, I walk in the dark, listening to the trees rustle and the occasional local dog barking at the shade-mad interloper walking too close to its house.

At many more times, though, I want light, yet still need or desire to be out at night. It might be the time of a new moon, or I may be traveling on unfamiliar trails. In such circumstances, I like a two-part solution.

One is a headlamp. Don't think of a miner, as the products available to the modern hiker are light, powerful, and elegant. I use a Black Diamond LED (light emitting diode) style—a model called Moonlight, shown in Figure 5-7— that costs about $30. The diodes reportedly last upward of seven years, and the life of three AAA batteries is about 7 hours at well below freezing, or more than 22 hours at room temperatures. It's bright enough to see the trail for walking, and light enough to be comfortable on the head.

In addition to the headlamp, I carry a flashlight. In part, it's a habit from scuba diving at night, where you always need a backup. Also, if you are caching, the flash can throw concentrated light where you want it most. Some people claim that the concentrated light helped them spot a cache at night— because of reflection—when they might have passed it over during the day. If you want a flashlight, get a good one that casts a clear and powerful beam. You can always play one-upmanship. I like Maglites and carry a tiny one, powered by a single AAA cell, on my key chain. I also have a larger one, using twin AA cells, that I sometimes bring along. Larger models can light a building and are heavy enough to club a small dinosaur into submission. You want to take extra batteries and a spare bulb, because you never know when something will go wrong. By the way, a pair of AA cells can sweetly fit into an old 35mm film canister.

Figure 5-7 Example of a headlamp
Photo courtesy of Black Diamond Equipment, Ltd.

I use Kodak and Fuji film, and for this purpose, like the former containers more; the Fuji brand caps fit into the canister, rather than on top, and make fitting the batteries difficult. A helpful convention I learned on the Geocaching.com discussion boards is to place the batteries positive side up if they are good and negative side up if they are dead.

Utilities

These are the things that you don't generally need, but can come in handy at the oddest times. I always have a knife when I'm hiking and geocaching. For that matter, I almost always have a knife on me, period—not some Bowie model the length of my forearm, but a combination job. This is an area where I've tried off-brands, and now I stick with the names. Swiss Army knives are an excellent choice, as are Leatherman combination tools. I currently have one of the former in my backpack, and a Victorinox combination with pliers, a knife blade, screw drivers, and other assorted handy items. Then there is the tiny Leatherman Micra on my keychain, along with the small flashlight; the scissors have many times over been worth the extra weight in my pockets.

If you need to signal in the case of an emergency, or simply want to find someone else in your party should you become separated, bring a whistle. Good models can be heard a long distance away.

Sometimes you will need cord—to lash something, to thread through a boot and replace a lace (why bring two things when one will do?), maybe to rig a cache in a place few people would think of looking. A hank of parachute cord 10 meters long, or about 33 feet, is strong and light.

I like to carry two bandanas. They are jacks-of-all-trades. You can improvise a splint with them and a stick, use them to cushion the chafe of a rope on tree bark, wet them and drape them on your head to stay cool, wipe sweat off your face, or even blow your nose.

Toilet paper is another handy item, and not just for the obvious reason. (Though don't discount the obvious. What convinced me to keep a roll was a time out in the woods, looking for a cache, when some coffee unexpectedly caught up with me. I had a couple of tissues, but a roll of TP would have been more comforting in an uncomfortable situation.) When threading your way through the brush, if you feel the need to mark your trail, tying strips of toilet paper to bushes or trees can guide you back. Yet in the next storm, your markers will begin to naturally decompose, and not exhibit the half-life of plastic trail tape.

Speaking of long rolls of material, duct tape is another standby. It can offer a field repair of almost anything from boot to shoulder strap. Don't fret over the size and weight of the rolls you see in a hardware store; simply create your own roll of a useful amount around a pencil. Doing this compresses the size of the bundle considerably and gives the pencil double duty.

The Elements

Anyone who will be out in the elements should take some standard items. If it's bug season, bring repellent. No reason why geocaching should be reduced to *buzz, ouch, slap, buzz, ouch, slap*. Lip balm can keep your mouth from cracking in winter's dry air. Also bring sunscreen. You might associate it with summer, but remember that you can still get a burn in the winter; the snow can act like a reflector, multiplying the effect of the sun, even if it is weaker than in summer.

The reflection of sun off snow can not only make you squint, but literally give you snow blindness, which means that you won't be able to see. Bring sunglasses to avoid this problem. Some experienced folk suggest a second pair, in case you lose the first. Those of us with prescription lenses might have trouble forking out the extra charge, so include an eyewear leash—one of those straps that fit onto the ends of the temple pieces and run around your neck—so the glasses stay put.

In some parts of the country, especially up in mountains, weather can change faster than human whim. Extra clothes are a prerequisite here. Bring some cold-weather gear if there's a chance that a pleasant time geocaching might turn chilly. When I'm out in cold weather, I often wear one of the synthetic long-sleeved t-shirts I mentioned, or a long underwear top. Next goes on the Gore-Tex shell, along with hat and gloves if needed. I carry the liner separately, because I don't want to overheat, yet still want to remain warm if I slow down, like when I'm at the end of my cache search, checking inside old logs or peering behind rocks.

Unexpected Events

Unexpected weather can lead to other unexpected things. If, heaven forbid, you become caught on a mountain and are unable to head back (due to either lack of light or concern about someone who is injured), another category of items comes into play. Fire is important to melt snow and ice for water, for cooking food, for staying warm, and for alerting search parties. Lighting a fire is not something you do for amusement or atmosphere.

If you do need to make a fire, you need fuel. In most areas, it's relatively easy to find sticks and branches. What may come harder are the materials to light that wood in the first place. Forget about rubbing two sticks together; stay practical. Into your kit of gear goes some waterproof and windproof matches. You will also need tinder if you want to make the transition from lit match to crackling fire. An expert I spoke with suggested two commonly available items. Candle stubs offer great tinder, if you shave slices off the candle and feed them to the growing blaze. The other component is lint from a clothes dryer; just fluff it up before use. Both these are items that will fit into 35mm film canisters (and yes, there are more things you can fit into 35mm canisters yet to come).

Something else that will keep you warm, and that I hope I never need, is a space blanket. These featherweight metallic foil sheets reflect 80 to 90 percent of your body heat back at you. This can save your life if you are stuck in frigid conditions without a proper tent and sleeping bag, or if you are injured and in shock. A variation on the blanket is a sack made of the same material. It is better at keeping you warm, but I opt for the regular version, because it is easier to wrap someone in a sheet than it is to stuff the body into a bag. In a pinch, a space blanket can also act as a windbreaker or signaling device.

NOTE You carry equipment and material for your own safety and use, if it is necessary. But we all have responsibilities beyond ourselves. Everyone should be prepared, but some aren't. So you must be ready to either help yourself, or help someone else if you are in the position to do so.

You know to carry rain gear, and perhaps cold-weather gear, depending on the location and time of year. But extra clothes, especially if you run the chance of getting soaked (such as searching around a river or hiking through wet snow), can be a smart move. At the least, I carry a dry pair of socks in a Ziploc bag. Getting your feet dripping wet is a vocational hazard. If your feet do become soaked, the best solution is to drop the boots, replace the socks with the dry pair, and put your boots back on. That will dry the boots from the inside out. This became more than theory when a cache hunt took me into a fetid swamp for about three hours. After sloshing through water for an extended period of time—some of which was spent up to my hips, with my boots stuck in mud—my gaiters gave up and I had no protection from water. By the time I got out, not only was I totally soaked from the waist down, but my hiking socks must have weighed literally several pounds each. It was an indescribable relief to shed them into a plastic bag, pour the water out of my boots, and then don the new socks. Sure, they got wet from the boots, but my footgear is still hearty, and my feet were happy.

At times, you or someone with you will get a cut, scrape, blister, or some other minor requirement for first aid. Although there is a bit more about the issue in Appendix B, it's wise to carry some select supplies. Here are some items you should consider keeping in a first aid kit:

- Antiseptic

- Bandages (an assortment of sizes)

- Burn cream

- Sting relief

- Sterile pads

- Pain relief (acetaminophen or ibuprofen; avoid aspirin, which can exacerbate bleeding)

- Benadryl (for allergic reactions)

- Moleskin (blisters)

- Tweezers

A first aid manual is also good, but it is best if you look through it before you ever need it; when in an emergency situation in unfamiliar surroundings, you are more likely to delay actions or make a mistake. Appendix A gives some sources for outdoor first aid courses, should you get ambitious. Note that regular first aid classes will often be of little help, because they assume that you have access to particular items, or that you can summon help. First aid outdoors often requires improvisation that must be practiced in advance.

All this is a collection of standard items for hikers. But why would most geocachers need it? Remember that you can easily spend an hour or more on even the simplest cache hunt, particularly when the hiding goes more smoothly than the seeking. That is why you also carry something to eat and drink.

Food and Water

Water could be the single most important thing you can carry to protect your health. As Appendix B explains, you can become dehydrated in hot weather or cold, dry weather or wet. If you will be out for two to three hours, bring 2 quarts or liters of water. You could go to a backpacking store and buy bottles ranging from 16 to 32 ounces (.5 to 1 liter), and even containers that hold 3 to 4 quarts or liters. Nalgene is the brand name of a rigid bottle used widely by hikers. You don't get the high amount of plastic smell in the water that you do with cheaper equipment, and you can get adapters that fit into the bottle tops and convert them into a smaller opening for convenient drinking. Then again, for most caching, you could use bicycle water bottles, or even sports-type water bottles from a grocery store. You can also get fancy with a hydration system—basically a backpack that has a water reservoir and a tube. You drink as you walk without having to fish a bottle out of your pack. Figure 5-8 shows one from Gregory Mountain Products, one of the familiar brands in this type of equipment.

Figure 5-8 Hydration system
Photo courtesy Gregory Mountain Products.

It's possible that you will run out of water. No one can carry all the water necessary for an extended hike. If you will be back quickly enough, then suffer through the dryness for a brief period. Otherwise, you will need to get water from the wild and purify it. The cheapest way of purifying water is to boil it, but this can be impractical, especially if you don't have a camp stove and pot. Another method is to use water purification tablets, which are usually a variation of iodine. Get the type that also comes with tablets (ascorbic acid) that neutralize the flavor, leaving the water somewhat palatable. You could also get an advanced camping water filter, if you are willing to spend the money, and if you are off in the wilderness often enough and away from ready sources of water, it is worth every penny and ounce. General Ecology makes portable water purifiers that meet the U.S. EPA standards for removing disease bacteria, viruses, and common problem cysts like giardia. The company's First Need purifier is meant to be carried (under a pound in weight), can purify almost two quarts/liters per minute, and even has optional adapters for a CamelBak hydration system.

If you drink only when you are thirsty, then you are already behind what your body needs. To avoid dehydration, you should be sipping regularly; the average person needs something like a gallon of water, from drinking as well as food, a day. This doesn't count coffee or alcohol, both of which could dry you out more. (For more on dealing with water, or a lack of it, see Appendix B.)

My favorite part of preparing for geocaching or hiking is knowing that I should bring food. It's great to have an official excuse to eat. There are two major goals in this. One is to have enough fuel to keep your body working. If you are out for hours, you can build up a considerable appetite. The other point of the food is electrolytes. If you don't have enough sodium and potassium, you can experience muscle pain and considerably worse, as Appendix B explains. Take in electrolytes, though, and you don't need to worry. Lightly salted trail mix—nuts and dried fruit—gives your body what it needs. If you don't or can't eat nuts, add a little salt to some dried fruit alone. Don't like the fruit? Eat nuts by themselves.

You can also find commercially prepared snacks that offer the calories and electrolytes. PowerBar is an easily found name in this genre, and I typically carry a couple for those times that I'm dragging. Look at the ingredients carefully, though, because some of the variations don't have significant amounts of potassium.

Niceties

Some items you don't really need, but might really want. A digital camera lets you record your progress and take any images that might be required by a cache owner. Some of the cameras I've seen are tiny and light, able to fit easily into a shirt pocket.

I also bring a set of compact binoculars to look at trees, birds, and far landscapes. You might want one of the many regional field guides available so you can identify flora or fauna. An item that has taken up residence in my traveling kit is a small star locator; when I'm out away from city lights on a clear night, I can look up, consider, and think. Outdoor stores sometimes have these; if your local one doesn't, go to science catalog company Edmund Scientifics (`www.scientificsonline.com`).

On a cold day, you might enjoy a warm drink to celebrate a find or a new cache hidden. You can bring along something hot in a vacuum container, or, instead, take a small camping stove, a pot, camping cups, some tea bags, honey, and lemon. There are few better tastes in the world than a hot cup of tea outdoors.

Packs

You have this entire assemblage of paraphernalia sitting before you; now you need somewhere to put it. The best choice is a day pack like the one shown in Figure 5-9.

Figure 5-9 Example of a day pack
Photo courtesy Gregory Mountain Products.

Day packs range from 1,500 to 2,000 cubic inches (20 to 25 liters). If you stick to tame local parks, or the occasional well-behaved state park, this size would more than suffice, as you should be able to carry enough to spend hours out. For hard caches that require real backpacking, you need a frame pack, either internal or external. The volumes can vary greatly, as can the features. In general, a hip belt bears most of the weight. Figure 5-10 shows a typical internal-frame pack.

Some frame packs load through the top, and others load through panels that open at the back. Check the references in Appendix A for books with additional information on true backpacking, such as correct loading methods.

Even a day pack should be carefully assembled. Be sure that the things you need most often are at the ready. That means stow the water bottle in a side pocket, or, better yet, in a holder on the pack designed to let you reach back and grab it while on the move. If you are out at night, have spare batteries and bulbs accessible, not buried under a mass of things that will be useless if you cannot see your hand in front of you. Keep the bulk of weight low and close to your back to avoid creating a burden that you will constantly fight.

Figure 5-10 Example of an overnight frame pack
Photo courtesy Gregory Mountain Products.

Geostuff

Aside from all the things demanded by a walk in the woods, you have the additional gear needed for geocaching.

Think your flashlight needs batteries? Ever had your digital camera run out of juice? Find that inconvenient? Try seeing your GPS system going out suddenly. It is imperative that you take extra batteries with you. It is common for your GPSr's batteries to give up the ghost at the most inconvenient times. Again, find one of your trusty film canisters for stowing them.

You need a collection of goodies for potential swapping when you find the cache. These should vary in size, so that you can leave something if you want, no matter what the size of the cache.

Make sure you print out a copy of the cache description, as well as any maps or other research information you might have gleaned from the Web. The next chapter discusses this more. You will probably also want a notepad and pen.

Do pack some resealable plastic food bags: sandwich, quart, and gallon size. If a bag in a cache is leaking, you can be kind and replace it. Also, these bags are great for such uses as storing your extra pair of socks or keeping a map dry, so you can double-up if necessary.

Garbage bags are helpful if you are going to trash out after caching in. I'd strongly suggest that you buy a package of disposable plastic gloves and keep a couple in your pack. After all, do you know where that stuff has been lately?

Environment

When out geocaching, you will, unfortunately, come across ample evidence that many people treat parks, forests, and remote wilderness areas as an extension of their garbage cans. Making use of those garbage bags you brought is important and the first step in living harmoniously with the environment you are visiting: cache in, trash out.

The catch phrase is *low impact*; you and others should not trample the world about you. For geocachers, the first principle is to stay on trails. When looking for a cache, there can be an enormous temptation to save time and immediately go cross country because the GPSr is saying, "It's that way, dummy." Realize, though, that responsible cache hiders don't generally go far off a trail, and that being smart sometimes means taking what seems to be the wrong way (more on this in Chapter 6). For really low impact, staying on a trail means just that, even when mud and water are in the way. It's tempting to move to the side, but if you are adequately equipped (you did bring those gaiters, didn't you?), the amount of moisture will prove no challenge. Just think of yourself as an overgrown child who has just been told not to get messy, and have some fun.

Try geocaching with small groups, not large. Large groups tend to spread out and do more damage. They are also noisier, and peace and tranquility are two qualities often missing in most of life, so why diminish them here, too? Actually, as far as I've seen, most geocachers go out either by themselves or in groups of two to four. But there are occasional *geoevents*, where cachers meet at particular coordinates, and at those times you should keep aware of impact.

If you find that you must "use the facilities" in a place that has none, the accepted approach these days is to dig a cathole 6 to 8 inches deep and 200 feet or 60 meters from any water sources, camp sites, or trails, then to bury the waste after you are done. (Good thing you brought that toilet paper.) If you will be out long enough that such personal business is likely to be necessary, add a small trowel to your pack, though check with local authorities about the potential problems of digging, even for a hasty privy.

On the Move

All this preparation, planning, and assembling of gear is so you can head out and geocache. One other step, though, is reminiscent of the joke about how to get to Carnegie Hall. No, the answer is not programming the WGS84 coordinates into your GPS and driving there; it's practice, practice, practice.

You don't want your time on the trail to be a painful learning experience. Try all your gear ahead of time and be sure you know how everything works. If you might find yourself in a position that would require making a fire, practice in a safe location at home, so you get a feel for how to feed the lint and candle shavings, move into dried leaves and twigs, and then get to branches. If you want to snowshoe to a cache, first try some snowshoeing by itself to get a sense of how to do it. Welcome your mistakes so you can learn from them.

Finally, you will be out on the trail. (OK, so you probably went right out on the trail when you bought your GPSr, but it's never too late to start hiking smartly.) You will soon figure out how to swing your day pack onto and off of your back. You can always prop your walking stick against a tree or rock wall to make it easier to pick up after a stop. If you don't have a ready prop, roll the stick with one foot onto your other and a little flip will have it into your hand.

Be wary of dangling anything as you walk, especially lanyards, and particularly GPSr lanyards. As you walk with the receiver in your hand, the cords have a persistently annoying habit of trying to embrace nature by getting tangled on any handy bush, branch, or rock. If you aren't careful, you could produce a fine imitation of a steer being roped and thrown at a rodeo.

Find your rhythm and adjust your stride to maintain it as the terrain changes. In other words, don't make your feet move more slowly as you are going uphill. Instead, shorten your stride on the upgrade but keep the pace. Always look before you leap, or step. Snow can cover thin ice or holes in the ground. Talus, a slope of rock debris at the base of a cliff, can be hidden by just enough topsoil and vegetation to keep you from realizing how easily you could lose your footing and begin a rapid descent. Remember, too, that this shouldn't become a forced march; you are not Caesar crossing the Rubicon. It's fine to rush off and back again if the hike isn't too far, but if you are on the chase of a difficult cache, use the backpacker's trick of taking a break of ten minutes out of every hour. If you aren't having fun, there is something wrong.

All this thankfully becomes second nature quite quickly, and you can enjoy your time in the woods, on a mountainside, and on the hunt for a cache.

On the Hunt

"Whatever we have got has been by infinite labour, and search,
and ranging through every corner of nature . . ."—Jonathan Swift

Now it's time to get down to caching business. Everything else until now has been preparation. Who said that running around in the woods while trying to find something was easy? It takes effort to run down a cache in the best way possible. After all, anything worth doing is worth doing well.

To learn more about hunting caches, you should remember the general steps from Chapter 2:

1. Go to a geocaching Web site and identify a cache you want to find.

2. Prepare for the search.

3. Go to the location.

4. Find the cache and make a note in its log book.

5. Enter your results on the cache Web page.

Then it's time to sit back and admire your conquest—until it's time for the next. Let's start with identifying the cache.

Identify the Cache

You can think of deciding which cache to pursue as a series of steps that narrows the field. The fundamental choice is location, the specific area where the cache sits. This doesn't necessarily mean where you live. You could decide on caching where you work, near the gym you attend, or behind your kid's school.

Vacation can also be a time for geocaching. So the first step is to match where you will be with a selection of caches.

Choosing by Location

Depending on where you are and what Web service you use, picking a cache by location can be easier or harder. At Geocaching.com for example, you can enter a postal code from the United States, Canada, the United Kingdom, or Australia and find caches without a given distance. In other areas, you must provide longitude and latitude, which can be found on topographic maps and at a number of Web sites, which I have listed in Appendix I. Navicache.com supports only U.S. zip code searches.

A useful feature on both Navicache.com and Geocaching.com is the ability to specify a distance from the location you pick, so you get all the caches located within that circle. Another welcome capability on Geocaching.com is a keyword search of the cache titles, as long as the word you specify is at least four letters long; otherwise, the search function says that there were no matches. This gets away from the location-centric type of decision, where you choose what is available near you, and opens the possibility of finding a set of caches that might be interesting, but that could require travel. For example, Figure 6-1 shows part of Geocaching.com's advanced search screen.

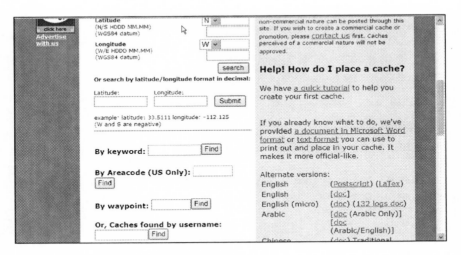

Figure 6-1 Geocaching.com search by keyword

To find all the cache names mentioning the word scuba, you enter the word and click the Find button. When I tried, only a few appeared, and none in my state.

Keyword searches can be tricky, because a word that one person might use may be missing from another's title. For example, I did a second search on Geocaching.com using *underwater* as the keyword. A completely different set of caches appeared. One made clear that it required scuba gear, although it did not use the term. Another actually had the word scuba in the instructions, but only for the cache owners to compliment the quality of diving in the area, and not because prolonged time submerged was necessary.

TIP Searching titles only can be limiting. To search everything, you can use a cute trick with Google.com. Say that you wanted to find all appearances of the word *scuba* on Geocaching.com, no matter where it appeared. In the Google search window, type **site:geocaching.com scuba**. That will return every page with the term scuba. Similarly, to get all the pages with scuba on Navicache.com, type **site:navicache.com scuba** in the Google.com window.

Many people like to group caches and find several during a single outing; in this case, a map search might be helpful. As Chapter 2 mentioned, Buxley's Geocaching Waypoints is one service. Geocaching.com put mapping in around the time of writing, and I've found that each has strengths and weaknesses, and that I like them for different things. Buxley's doesn't always indicate on a timely basis when caches are archived (made unavailable). But it does let you drill down on a geographic basis from the start of your search. Geocaching.com lets you select a cache and then click the *View Map* link that creates a map of the surrounding area, along with nearby caches. Both let you zoom in and out (though Geocaching.com can zoom in closer). So if I am going to be in an area unfamiliar to me, or I was using Navicache.com and wanted a map, I'd probably use Buxley's first to determine what was around. If I decided on a specific cache, then I'd use Geocaching.com's mapping to find what else I might pick up. Different tools, different uses.

NOTE Geographic efficiency can be highly desirable. A geocacher in Montana searches for caches only occasionally because the number near him is limited. He tells a story of going after three caches in one day—and driving hundreds of miles to do so. For some people, adding a chauffeur to the gear list might not be a bad idea.

If you were going to visit South Portland, Oregon, and wanted to go geocaching, you could go to Buxley's and click through the world and U.S. maps to reach the map for Oregon, as shown in Figure 6-2.

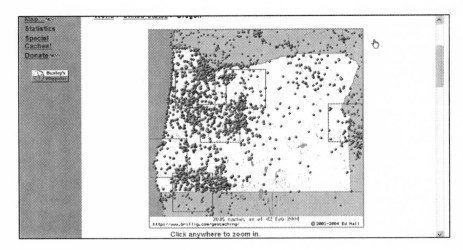

Figure 6-2 Oregon cache map

Notice that the site is prompting you to zoom in on the South Portland region. (Don't click on one of the balls, or you will immediately go to the page for that particular cache.) Figure 6-3 shows caches in the area, allowing the geocaching traveler to better plan outings.

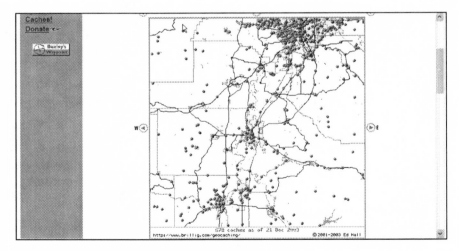

Figure 6-3 Caches in the South Portland, Oregon region

Location, however, is just one part of choosing a cache.

Taking Suggestions

Other sources for caches are available. One is geocaching organizations. Many regions have groups of geocachers who get together and trade information. Some even maintain electronic newsgroups to keep each other informed. The major geocaching sites also have discussion forums with geographic sections. Talk to people in your area, or in the area to which you will be traveling, and seek their opinions. Especially when visiting an unfamiliar area, ask if there are any "must do" caches that would be the most enjoyable use of your time.

Also look at the personal Web pages people maintain for geocaching. Occasionally, you will find some with caches unavailable anywhere else. No, you don't get the points you rack up at the geocaching sites, but you get to see something most people never will. Some people also set up private caches available only to friends and family. To discover those, patience, luck, and a good personality are your best allies.

Finding Your Level

The next step is to look at the difficulty and terrain ratings and consider what might make sense for what you want to do. The first thing the ratings will do is suggest how long it might take to find the cache. Once you get to the general location and park your car, a cache with a 1 difficulty rating should take a few minutes to perhaps half an hour to find. With a rating of 2, it might take an hour. This progresses to a 5 rating, which can take all day or even an overnight stay, or mean that you'd better sharpen your puzzle-solving skills. The terrain at a 1 might be paved or smooth, hard-packed trails over which you could even roll a wheelchair. By the time you get to a 5, you could well need technical climbing gear, scuba equipment, a kayak, or other specialized paraphernalia.

Time is a definite factor, as are expertise and preparation. If you are interested in a casual geocaching experience (a good choice at the beginning), then go for a low-rated cache. Conversely, if a high-rated cache catches your fancy, be sure that you know how to approach it. Suddenly deciding to scuba dive 100 feet or scale a granite wall for a clue in a multi-cache without spending time learning how to do it correctly could leave you dead in the blink of an eye.

You also must consider whether a cache is appropriate for people going with you. This is particularly true if they are children. What might seem a moderate walk and acceptable time looking for a container could be too long for the younger set. There is no sense in making a miserable time for all by selecting a cache that might be beyond the stamina, patience, or attention span of some.

Gauging Your Interest

Aside from convenience and practical considerations, the cache should sound fun to pursue. This is an easier hurdle for those new to the activity, because everything is novel. As time goes on, you might find that low-rated caches are too easy. Some people enjoy particular types of caches, like multis. This is where the description becomes particularly useful. Do you really enjoy the swapping part of caching? If so, a virtual cache might be a secondary choice compared to one that could expand your loot collection. Some enjoy caches with historical connections. The descriptions can provide guidance to potential problems, help alert you to specific conditions, and, most importantly, detail the rules of the cache.

Every cache owner has the right and opportunity to determine what a finder must do to claim credit for a particular cache. Some will demand digital photos, others might request that only particular types of items be placed into the cache. The owner may require that you e-mail particular information gained during your hunt to keep a claim to a cache. If you are not going to honor the rules, choose another cache. This is supposed to be enjoyable for everyone involved.

Setting Alerts

Both `Geocaching.com` and `Navicache.com` provide facilities to watch or spy on a cache. This means that any activity of people finding the cache or posting notes about it is e-mailed directly to you. This can alert you to changes in the cache that might affect your decision to go after it. Figure 6-4 shows, toward upper right, an example of the link to watch the cache from `Navicache.com`.

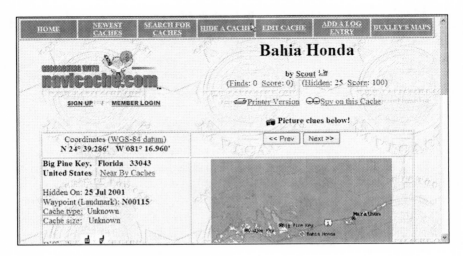

Figure 6-4 Examples of cache watching

You might choose a particular cache because you noticed that it is holding a hitchhiker, and you've always wanted to stumble across one. If you plan to go on your hunt later in the week, you don't want to find that someone beat you to the cache, taking the hitchhiker, which might cause you to change your plans. By receiving activity updates, you can see if someone reported having taken the hitchhiker before your expected foray. You would also be notified if someone traveled to the cache and thought that the container might have been stolen (which happens occasionally).

There are other reasons to use a watch or spy list. On Geocaching.com, it's possible to keep tabs on a travel bug and follow its progress. I also recently found another circumstance. There was a multi that I and several other cachers had been unable to find. It seems that the first stage went missing before anyone could find it. The cache owner placed a note to say that it would be replaced. Now I will be informed when it is, so I can make another attempt.

So now that you have an idea of how to pick a cache, it's time to move on to the next step. Although many people think that fun should be carefree, I've found that the best fun comes after proper preparation.

Prepare for the Search

You know where you want to go; now you need to plan how to get there and back again. The first step is to assemble the cache information, gather information for getting to the cache, then pull together everything (and everyone) you will need and plan your approach.

Assemble the Cache Information

The natural starting point for information is the cache Web page. You may find clues written in code in either Geocaching.com or Navicache.com. Both generally have spots to click to decode the hints. In general, it's easier to do that, then print the cache page and fold it so that the clue is hidden behind the main description. If you are concerned that you will give in to temptation too easily, leave the clue encrypted. All the cache pages with encrypted clues have translation tables, though it will take some time. Figure 6-5 shows an example of an encrypted clue and its translation table.

One of the most important things to remember is to bring the cache page with you. Otherwise, Murphy's Law almost guarantees that you'll end up wishing you had brought some pertinent information that might make all the difference between finding a cache or going home in defeat. This is certainly easier than calling friends from your cell phone and pleading that they check the Web page for the clues and read them to you. It's much less embarrassing, too.

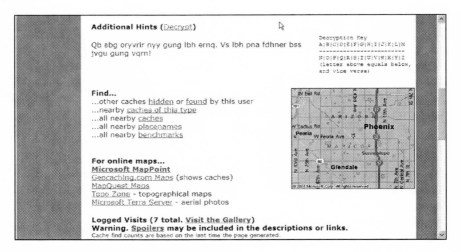

Figure 6-5 An encrypted clue on a Web page

While you are at the cache page, take another read through and see if anything described needs additional research. For example, I've found myself checking on the Web for images of plants and trees if they are mentioned in a description. Is a cache at the edge of a drumlin? Best to know what a drumlin is.

Get Your Navigation Information

Finding the cache will be difficult if you don't know where you are headed, so you need to enter the cache coordinates into your GPSr. You can do this manually by creating a waypoint and altering the coordinates.

There is another way, however. Geocaching.com supports EasyGPS. This program, from a company called TopoGrafix, lets you manage waypoints and move them between your computer and GPSr. Point a browser to www.easygps.com to download your free copy. Once you have downloaded and installed the program, here is how to use it:

1. Direct a browser to the page of the cache you want to find.

2. Click on the link to download the coordinates.

3. When prompted, click the Save button.

4. Choose a location for the file and click Save again.

5. Start your copy of EasyGPS. You will see the screen in Figure 6-6.

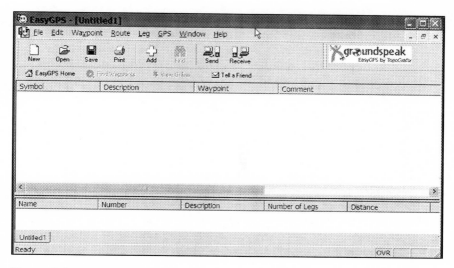

Figure 6-6 EasyGPS screen

6. Click the Open button and find the file with the coordinates.

7. Connect your GPSr to your PC and turn the PC on.

8. Right-click the cache and select Send Waypoint to GPS, as in Figure 6-7.

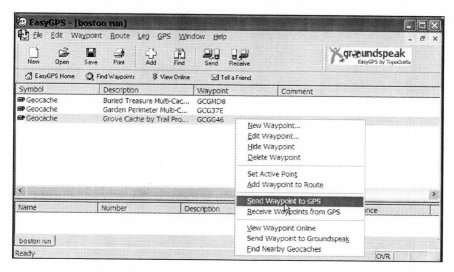

Figure 6-7 Sending the waypoint to the receiver

9. Turn off the GPSr and disconnect it, then close EasyGPS.

I like to keep a running track of the caches that I'm planning to look for and those I've found. Caches that I've found I save into a file called My Geocaching. When I download additional caches, I do so to a separate file, then download the coordinates to my GPSr. After I (hopefully) find the caches, I go back to EasyGPS and then open My Geocaching, leaving EasyGPS showing two tabs at the bottom. One of them will be the downloaded file that I opened, and the other, My Geocaching. I click the tab for the downloaded caches, highlight them, and press Ctrl-C to copy them. Then I click on the My Geocaching tab and press Ctrl-V to paste those in with the others.

I also make use of the different icons available. When I find a cache, I start EasyGPS, open My Geocaching, go to the cache name, right-click it, and choose Edit Waypoint. Going to Symbol, I can choose any icon, including Geocache (a closed treasure chest) and Geocache Found (the chest opened).

> **NOTE** Although I describe EasyGPS, which I had used it for some time, I eventually graduated to one of the pay versions of TopoGrafix's software. There are two choices: PanTerra and ExpertGPS. I skipped right to the latter. You get many waypoints of navigational reference points—at least in the United States—as well as online USGS topographic maps that make planning your assault on a cache easier to manage. If you are a premium member at Geocaching.com, you can also run something called a pocket query, which allows you to build a list from 100 to 500 caches specifying such things as the number of miles from a point you specify, whether or not you own the cache, and whether or not you have found it. You can have the information sent to you in a LOC file, which is the type that TopoGrafix uses, or you can choose GPX, which is a type supported by a growing number of GPS-related applications from different vendors.

Although you can download a waypoint from the cache page, you can also download more than one at once. Do a search for caches near a location. In the resulting list, each will have a download check box at the end. Check the ones you want, then scroll to the bottom of the page and click Download to EasyGPS.

Because this is specifically about Geocaching.com, you should remember that when you search for caches near a particular location, you see them listed by distance and direction from that point. However, the sorting is done by distance, so two adjacent caches on the list could actually be in completely opposite directions. The way to determine how to effectively group caches is to use a map.

Both Geocaching.com and Navicache.com have links to maps. Geocaching.com brings up an appropriate selection from a variety of map sources (Microsoft MapPoint, MapQuest, Topo Zone, Microsoft Terra Server, and Rand McNally), whereas Navicache.com has a built-in map with five levels of zooming permitted. Geocaching.com's View Map link will display a map with zooming features that shows surrounding caches and any travel bugs in any of those caches. Both of the geocaching sites also have links to topographic maps and aerial photography. If the services they use are not your preferred sources, you can always go to a mapping site and provide the lat/lon coordinates. Appendix I provides some other resources.

> **NOTE** The maps at TopoZone and other topographic map services stand a good chance of using some datum other than WGS84. To use the map for more than general guidance, make sure that you change the datum in your GPSr to the appropriate datum, remembering to switch it back to WGS84 before you next download a cache waypoint.

For absolute safety, it would be wise to make two copies of all the information you create and leave them with someone. That way, should you not turn up when expected, someone can tell the authorities where you went.

I must say, though, that with safety and intelligence in mind, I still most often go out caching alone. It may be foolish—I've gone solo backpacking, too, and know that is at odds with generally accepted prudence—but I yearn for the solitude, the chattering of dried leaves under foot, the smell of pine and cedar, the heat of a summer's sun or, contrarily, a chill so profound that it seems to start just under my skin. Could I get into trouble? Most assuredly, and those who travel with others will have fewer problems. I don't know that I could be happy without the aloneness, however.

To avoid needless complications, whether heading out solo or en masse, it is intelligent to do some additional research before departing.

Important Background

It is clear that if you are going someplace new, especially an area requiring you to travel a distance, it would be sensible to know some things in advance. Here are some fundamental questions you should ask:

- How close can I drive to the ultimate cache location?

- Can I park nearby?

- Are there specific hours of operation or access?

- Do I need permission to enter, or is there a fee for use?

- Are there any seasonal use restrictions?

- What is the weather likely to be?

- Will I need special gear? If so, can it be rented, or must I bring my own?

- Is the spot appropriate for any of my other outdoor hobbies, either before or after the hunt?

Once I was in a state park on a whim for nothing more than a hike. The park was home to some caches, though I wasn't caching at the time. As I drove to the parking area, a sign indicated that the park would be closed for a week of deer hunting season. Had I actually been planning to go caching and my timing been off, I could have arrived at a time when it would have been unsafe to venture into the woods. Because I live only a short distance from this park, this would have been only an inconvenience. However, if I had traveled for a special caching trip only to be turned away by circumstances, I would have been aggravated at the least. Don't depend on good fortune; it's much easier to schedule a phone call or to visit a Web site for information that might make a difference to your caching travel plans.

Gather Ye Sundries While Ye May

You know where you are going and how to get there. Now it's time to pull together everything you need. Check Chapter 5 for the items you might want to bring along, from water and food, to a change of clothing, compass, and walking stick. Consider anything your research indicated might be warranted. Be sure to bring the geostuff. You might include some of the following:

- Extra pad and pencil, in case a cache is missing a log

- Garbage bags: one to put in the cache for others to use, and another to do some cleaning while you are there

- Extra plastic bags

- Extra pens

Now it is time to consider what items you might want to leave in the cache.

Choosing Goodies to Leave

Picking something to leave in a cache is a process of balancing factors of size, cache themes, ingenuity, and personal style. This is one of those times when size becomes critical. Cache descriptions often mention the container's size. Things that barely fit into a gallon container or a big ammo box won't nestle into a small box. In some cases, the cache Web page won't indicate the container's size; this is when you should either think small or bring a variety of possible items.

When a cache has a theme, work with that. I remember one that was media-related and requested that all items be in keeping with the theme. Look at the cache's name and the items originally included by its owner, if mentioned on the cache page. See if you can find something that fits.

Goodies also vary in value. In some cases, some items may be worth real money (anything more than a couple dollars). A general caching ethos dictates that you leave something about equal in value to what you take. So try to bring a variety of items, from chintzy to chichi.

Making a good choice comes down to ingenuity. One common gripe among many cachers is that people leave old toys from fast food chains. (Did someone order the McGeo?) If you are going to take the trouble to find a cache, you might as well put an original spin on how you make your mark. A good part of this choice is personal style. I usually try to leave at item related to writing. That can be a pen, notebook, book mark, or something similar. When you set up an account on a geocaching Web site, you pick a name. Find something that touches on an interest, character trait, or other personal detail. Then consider a trademark item to leave.

There are items you should avoid because of impracticality or poor taste. Food is a bad choice for a cache swap. If it's not in a metal can, chances are good that enough smell might escape to attract an animal. The woodland critter could then eat through the container, causing permanent damage to the cache. Even if something seems sealed, who is going to trust food left by people they don't know? Just skip the PowerBars. Also forget anything that might be damaged by the handling or the weather it will have to bear. Authentic Fabergé eggs are probably a bad idea.

Also inappropriate are items too adult in nature. There have been a number of reports of prophylactics left in caches. Geocaching is a family activity, and many parents do not want to see their children open a package that forces them to provide an explanation that could have waited a few years (that is, if they can get past the stammering phase).

If you need to do something a little different, consider leaving something that will make its way from one cache to the next.

Traveling Cache Denizens

A far better fit is a hitchhiker, which is a way to express your creativity, or help someone else's. If you remember, a hitchhiker is an item that goes from cache to cache, often with some mission. (I recently picked up a "turtle" that was part of a race. The first to reach at least ten caches and return to its home cache would be the winner.) Some hitchhikers provide private cache coordinates that are unavailable any other way.

If you are handy with Web design and programming, you could set up an online page and ask that people finding the hitchhiker update its progress. Or you could use a travel bug, which is a commercial tag with serial number available from `Geocaching.com`. You place the tag, like an army dog tag, on an item and send it out. The service comes with a progress updating mechanism on the Web.

At some caches, however, you cannot leave anything.

Nontraditional Caches

Even multi-caches, with one stage leading to the next, generally culminate in a container with things for trading. In some nontraditional caches, though, there may be no place to leave anything. Virtual caches direct you to a spot, then ask for proof that you have been there and done that. You may need to collect information or take a picture of yourself and e-mail it to the cache owner for credit. An example of a basic virtual cache is A Basic Virtual, shown in Figure 6-8.

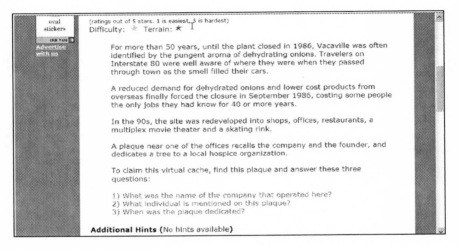

Figure 6-8 A virtual cache

In some cases, you must position yourself in a particular spot and wait for a webcam—a digital camera that periodically takes images and displays them on a Web site. For these you generally need a partner who is connected to you at the virtual hip by a cell phone and who has Internet access. Your partner saves the screen shot when the webcam finally takes a shot with you in the frame. This can take a while, so patience is advised.

> **NOTE** I've tested wireless Internet services. Most cellular providers have them. You could get such a service, bring your laptop computer, and stand there waiting for the proper image to show up. But that does seem a touch extreme, doesn't it? And what about the extra weight? A wireless PDA might seem a good idea, but grabbing an image on the tiny screen could leave the electronic evidence for claiming the find hard to see and therefore unconvincing.

The third type of "untouchy feely" cache is the locationless cache. For these, you look for a place that meets certain requirements. This might entail finding an arboretum, as in Arboretum Walkabout from Anton of Syracuse, New York, in the United States. (I'm planning to hightail it to the Arnold Arboretum in Boston to get my credit.) You may have to find an aqueduct built before the twentieth century, as specified in Ancient Aqueducts by geo-cacher MAntunes of Lisbon, Portugal. Who says you have to travel to reach international caches?

In general, a locationless cache allows only one credit per cacher and one credit per location. If you are going to attempt one, check the logs of the cache to be sure no one has beaten you to your intended spot.

By this time, no matter what type of cache you are seeking, it's time to hit the road.

Out on the Hunt

Now you are ready to go after your quarry. That means you have to do the following things:

- Get to the right area
- Find the actual cache
- Avoid the attention of strangers
- Safely retrieve the cache
- Make your log
- Replace the cache

During your first cache hunt, you may well find that these steps can be deceptively difficult.

Get to the Right Area

You have the cache waypoint, so now you must get to the right area. This can be an absolutely maddening prospect if you go about it the wrong way. Your prelim-inary research should show the geographic area in which the cache resides. But you must find a clear path for driving and parking. Sometimes the cache des-cription offers coordinates for parking, but often there is nothing. Finding a spot for your noble steed to sit and wait can be easier said than done.

I can remember once driving in circles on a cache hunt, not having both-ered to check maps. Instead, I was just using my GPSr to get what I thought would be reasonably close to the cache. After all, this was close to home and an area that I presumably knew. After moving this way and that, I saw a dirt road to my left entering a reservation area I had never before noticed. A quick turn in, and it seemed that I was on the way, under one-third of a mile from the spot. I went over the trails, then off, drawn by the GPSr. I kept going, soaking my shoes (having forgotten hiking boots) in a marsh, getting tangled in briars. Finally I was under one-tenth of a mile, just 400 feet, when I suddenly realized that the cache was straight ahead—on the other side of a river in a reserve in another town.

Always check the driving directions from the maps you have printed, and consider getting an area street map if available. Time searching is best spent looking for the actual cache, not a parking space. These days, I don't turn on the GPSr while driving if I can possibly avoid it until I'm close to parking. A few minutes before arriving, I switch it on and put it on the dash. That way, the receiver is usually ready to go when I am without wasting battery power.

> **NOTE** There may be multiple possible parking spots for a given cache; not all are likely to be equal. Some checking might indicate that one is farther removed from the cache than another. I often pick the farther parking as an excuse for a longer walk. If you are looking with children, or feeling particularly fatigued by one too many cache hunts in a single day, you might consider finding the closer one.

Depending on your familiarity with the area, you might turn on your GPSr while driving and use the goto function to navigate toward the cache waypoint; when the distance dips and then starts to rise again, you often find that you just passed your intended parking spot, because it is closest to the actual cache. As with all rules of thumb, this one can take you awry, but I've found it usually reliable. Once you are in the right area, it's time to start looking.

On the Scent

This is what you've been waiting for. If you didn't turn on the receiver while driving up, do it after you park the car so the GPSr can take up to a few minutes to lock on satellite signals and be ready to use. Before you run off, get your gear together. Save a waypoint for your current position; this can be critical for finding your way back to your car. I also reset the odometer or trip computer portion of my GPSr. Hiking and geocaching are part—the vast majority, come to think about it—of my exercise regime, and I like to monitor the distance I cover.

> **NOTE** Although you can geocache in virtually any weather, here are some practical considerations. All the units use liquid-crystal displays that can temporarily stop working in extreme cold—the crystals congeal and don't respond to the display signals. Keep the receiver in an inner pocket to keep it warm. However, don't become paranoid; I was able to complete two caches in 12° Fahrenheit (-10° Celsius) with no problem. The other issue is rain. Receivers are usually waterproof except for the battery compartments. In a light drizzle it is probably fine, but in heavier precipitation, operating it through a plastic bag is advisable.

Start moving, at whatever speed makes you comfortable, and follow the direction of your receiver. You will soon find one problem of GPS: it offers a straight-line direction from your location to the waypoint. Unfortunately, there is seldom a straight-line path in that direction. A bit of skill is necessary in here.

As you move along the trails, watch the direction suggested by the GPSr. You might find yourself traveling down one turn or part of a fork when you realize that the receiver's suggested direction indicates that another trail would have been better, as you can see in Figure 6-9.

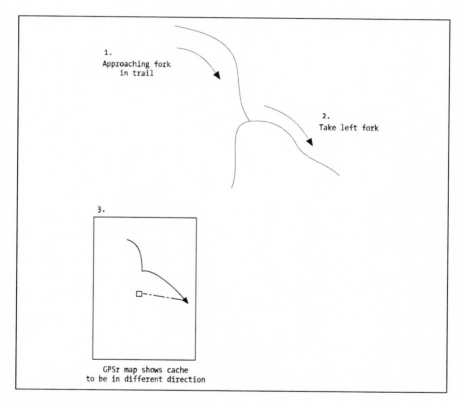

Figure 6-9 Trying to follow directions

In general, caches don't require you to go off the trail for a long distance, so when the cache appears to be completely off the trail, think twice. Most caches are likely within a couple hundred feet of a trail. Having to fight your way through significant obstructions is unusual, especially if the difficulty and terrain ratings are low.

Even if you are on the right trail, the GPSr reading can be deceiving. You might be walking on what seems to be the right trail and suddenly find the distance to the waypoint increasing. That doesn't mean you are on the wrong trail or that you have missed a turn off the trail. Look at Figure 6-10.

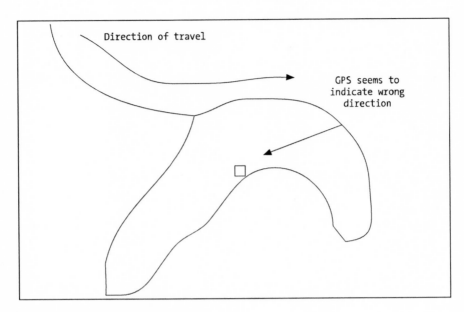

Figure 6-10 Avoiding GPSr confusion

The problem is that the receiver indicates a straight-line direction to the cache. Notice that the trail first moves away from the cache and then doubles back. From a consideration only of distance and not terrain, it would make sense to bushwhack directly. But that is a bad idea for two reasons. One is pure practicality: moving on an existing trail is far easier then going through brush. I've found that my pace drops by as much as two-thirds, or even comes to a complete halt, if I attempt this.

Staying on the established path as much as possible is also an ecologically responsible tactic. Every time you go off trail, you break branches, crush plants, and cause general destruction. Knowing when to leave the trail becomes a matter of experience. If my receiver indicated that I was a one-tenth of a mile (150 meters) away from the cache, I'd keep to the trail on the educated guess that the trail would move closer again, and that I would get closer in less time by following the path more traveled. Drop the distance to under 200 feet (60 meters) with the indicator sharply pointing away from the trail, and I'd eye the path to see if it bent in whatever direction I needed to go. If not, I'd consider heading off.

When you enter this "near zone," you need to alter your approach. No longer can you stride at your usual speed. Your position displayed by the GPSr is a combination of location and the device's calculations of your direction and how quickly you are moving. A rapid pace makes it appear as though you have arrived at the location before you really have, because it takes the receiver some time to realize that you have actually slowed down. Then, while standing still, the distance between you and the cache will appear to again grow as the GPSr reworks its calculations based on its new grasp of your position. Also, because consumer GPS has a potential error of up to 50 feet, it's best to entertain the possibility that the cache will not be exactly where the receiver and coordinates suggest. In fact, the potential for error between the cache owner's receiver and the seeker's amounts to a possible radius of 100 feet in which the cache might actually be. Luckily, the coordinates generally seem more accurate, but it's good never to become overly confident.

Find It

Often, it's the last 10 percent of any effort that is the hardest. This is when you cannot afford to drift. Make no mistake, that final cache search often requires the bulk of your energy and time, especially when you face cache owners who enjoy making things "interesting."

You have arrived at the coordinates, but the cache container is unlikely to be obviously placed. This is when some searching technique can be handy. You can classify this technique by three broad categories:

- Psychological
- Analytical
- Metaphysical

Some combination of the three should get you to any cache. Eventually. Well, most of the time.

Psychological

Many cachers go into a hunt trying to think like a cache owner. Certain types of hiding places make sense. Many cache pages mention the size and type of the container, and a space must be large enough to hold the container. Except for some older caches and the occasional one hidden in sand, caches are not buried underground. (Neither Navicache.com nor Geocaching.com will approve buried caches because of concern about damage to the environment.)

This means the hiding place will usually be obvious to some degree. Hollow trees, cavities under or between rocks, and spaces behind trees not exposed to the casual trail hiker are all potential candidates for cache hiding places.

The cache will also probably be partially or completely hidden. That gives a second clue, which is to look for something that seems like camouflage. You might see rocks piled against the base of a boulder in an unnatural way, or some large pieces of bark laid across some cavity. These are spots that smack of holding a cache.

Finding the likely spots quickly becomes easier as you search for more caches. Nevertheless, psychology can backfire. Some geocachers go to extreme lengths when hiding containers. Camouflage paint, to make them blend in, is a mild step. Some cachers have hollowed fake tree stumps, splitting off the top to act as a closely fitting lid. A Georgia cacher with the Geocaching.com handle "mrplug" had what he called The Smallest Cache in the World, which was inactive the last time I looked. For a sense of how hard it might be to find a cache, look at Figure 6-11.

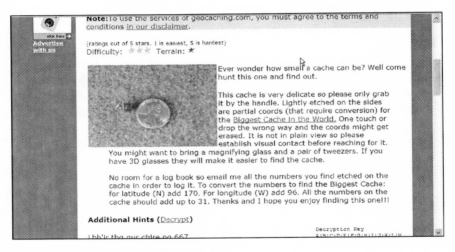

Note: To use the services of geocaching.com, you must agree to the terms and conditions in our disclaimer.

(ratings out of 5 stars. 1 is easiest, 5 is hardest)
Difficulty: ✶✶✶ Terrain: ✶

Ever wonder how small a cache can be? Well come hunt this one and find out.

This cache is very delicate so please only grab it by the handle. Lightly etched on the sides are partial coords (that require conversion) for the Biggest Cache in the World. One touch or drop the wrong way and the coords might get erased. It is not in plain view so please establish visual contact before reaching for it. You might want to bring a magnifying glass and a pair of tweezers. If you have 3D glasses they will make it easier to find the cache.

No room for a log book so email me all the numbers you find etched on the cache in order to log it. To convert the numbers to find the Biggest Cache: for latitude (N) add 170. For longitude (W) add 96. All the numbers on the cache should add up to 31. Thanks and I hope you enjoy finding this one!!!

Additional Hints (Decrypt)

Decryption Key
A:B:C:D:E:F:G:H:I:J:K:L:M

Lbb'ir tbq aur chire ng 667

Figure 6-11 The world's smallest cache?

This cache wasn't a container and didn't contain anything—it had a series of numbers engraved on the side. To get credit, you reported the digits back to the cache owner. According to some who found it, a magnifying glass was a good addition to your pack.

Some cache owners delight in surprising seekers more craftily. They place the caches in areas with some "obvious" hiding spots to draw attention. In some cases, these cache hiding candidates are not at the coordinates, but close enough that someone eager for a find might be diverted. I once actually created a multi in which the first stage was a bit tricky. People tended to check one obvious hiding spot when the real one, which appeared to be unable to hold the clue to the next stage, was only two inches away.

Analytical

Sometimes you won't be able to find the cache, even after exploring what seem to be the likely possibilities. Analytical skills come into play now. You must begin to reassess your approach.

One tool you can use is triangulation, a trick that I happily stole from Kelly Markwell's geocaching site (see the resources in Appendix I). Chapter 3 explains how the GPS system uses triangulation to identify location. You can use something similar with your receiver. Begin to walk slowly toward the cache location from one direction, and notice the line in which the receiver directs you. Mentally extend that line forward and pick out a landmark in the distance. (See Figure 6-12.)

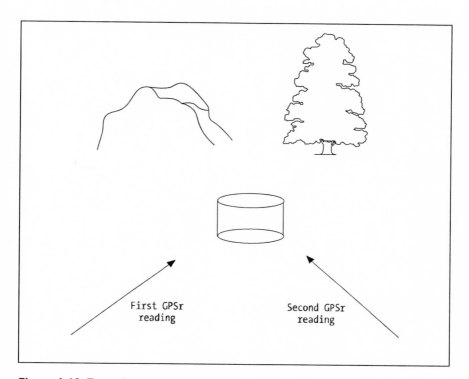

Figure 6-12 Triangulating a cache's position

Now, as the figure shows, approach from a different point and mentally note the direction again. Where the lines cross should be a likely candidate for finding the cache. Of course, your readings could be at odds with that of the person who hid the cache. But if finding a cache were an exact and predictable series of steps each time, geocaching would be boring.

Now is also the time to pay attention to the condition of the land around you. Look for signs of where people have previously gone: broken twigs and plants, bent grasses, impressions in snow or mud. Of course, they might lead you in the wrong direction.

> **NOTE** When trying to find the final stage of a multi-cache once, I could see someone's footprints about the ground. Suspecting who the person was (a highly experienced cacher), I followed his path for a time to different spots that seemed reasonable hiding places. But everywhere I went, there was no cache to be found. Eventually, I began to wonder whether he might not have missed the cache, so I started looking in less obvious places. Within another 15 minutes or so, I found it and learned by looking in the log book that I had been the first finder. Remember that the crowd is not always right.

Tools, too, have their limitations. Sometimes, your GPSr's reading will be significantly off. In such cases, there is little you can do but take the time to broaden your area of search or return for another try at a later time.

Metaphysical

This is an approach to caching that I must confess eludes me. But in the interest of those who might be more attuned, here it is. There are cachers who claim to tap into "the force." Somehow, they obtain some mystical sense of where the cache is. It may be one of those abilities that you either have or don't. If you feel your own magnetic draw to the right hiding places, more power to you.

When All Else Fails

At times, all of your work will not turn up a cache. That is why you take a print-out of the cache page with you. Now is the time to either unfold the hint or decrypt it. At what point you hit the need for a clue is up to you. If you are new at geocaching, there is no reason not to look at clues before you go on your first few hunts. Then again, if you have a low tolerance for frustration, look at the hints before searching for any cache. This is supposed to be fun, not an exploration of officially sanctioned and regulated activity.

> **NOTE** Even the cache owner's clue can fail you. There is nothing so frustrating in geocaching when you've gone through the river as well as the woods, been raked by briars, spent an hour looking in vain, and finally decrypted the clue only to find that it tells you to leave your car in the parking lot.

Opening the Prize

Ah, yes, there's even something to say about opening the cache once you have it. Within, there will likely be a number of items you can take, assuming that you leave something of your own as a replacement. Although you can swap any way you wish, the generally accepted ethos is to match the value of the cache item that you take.

If you are caching with kids, they will be excited to actually open the container. Be aware, however, that not all people cache with a general audience in mind. As mentioned before, some cachers have reported finding condoms in some containers. If you decide to let children open the cache, keep an eye over their shoulders so you can take control if necessary.

At times you will find items left in plastic bags to both protect against potential breach of the container and to keep items together. You must use common sense and experience to understand their functions and decide how to deal with them all. Generally, there will be a plastic bag containing a note explaining the cache and game (for those who find the container by accident) as well as a log and a pen or pencil, and sometimes a pencil sharpener. These must remain in the cache, though you need to fill in a page of the log with your caching handle, date of the find, and any notes or observations you wish.

The items for trade may at times be in their own bag. There might also be other bags that contain hitchhikers. You are free to take one of these, so long as you are willing to abide by the rules contained in the bag, which usually means moving the item to another cache in a timely manner. If you cannot do that, don't take the hitchhiker.

Occasionally, you will find such commemorative items as special business cards with the cache's name, pins, trading cards called *cachecards* (see Appendix I), and other items that you are encouraged to take and keep, or sometimes to help distribute as widely as possible. Again, use your common sense. If I see a collection of cards from many different areas, I assume that people left them for the cache owner and not as an item for others to remove.

Secrecy and Safety

While you look, keep in mind that geocaching is something of an underground sport. You don't want uninvolved people to start poking into, moving, or taking caches. If you see people around, don't actively search; wait until they pass. Privacy is a particular problem in urban geocaching, where what you seek might be in a heavily trafficked park or even on a city street.

You may have to abandon a search to protect a cache. In such cases, I continue on with a hike and enjoy the outdoors.

Sometimes people will notice your behavior and ask what you are doing. You can respond in a couple different ways. One is to dissemble, pretending to be doing something else. That seems pointless. I advocate open explanation. After all, geocaching is neither illegal nor destructive. Tell someone about it, and you might have found a potential new geocacher. If the person is in a position of authority, such as a policeman or park ranger, lying is a particularly bad idea.

You might even find that the inquiring person is another geocacher. That offers the chance to trade stories, tips, and opinions on good local caches.

The other overall consideration is safety. Test footing before you step out onto ice or a seeming smooth patch of ground covered in debris. (A walking stick is particularly good in this application.) If you need to check under a log or among rocks and you don't have a clear view of the interior, poke a stick in first so your hand doesn't make first contact with an alarmed animal.

Become familiar with identifying poison ivy, oak, and sumac. Many cachers have had such unexpected run-ins, which does nothing but increase the stock price of chamomile lotion manufacturers. Also, learn about biting insects: what to wear and what to coat your skin with to avoid looking like a relief map.

After you've gone hunting for a number of caches, you might get the itch to hide some of your own, which is what Chapter 7 will teach you.

In Hiding

"The height of cleverness is to be able to conceal it."—Francois de La Rochefoucauld

To many people, the fun in geocaching is in the hunt's thrill. But there is no chase without a quarry, and, luckily, many cachers find challenge in choosing locations and hiding containers. They might emphasize the actual visit to a beautiful spot or the challenge offered to the seeker, but all hiders get a dual satisfaction: providing for the enjoyment of others and exercising their cleverness.

As with finding a cache, it helps to remember the appropriate steps from Chapter 2 when hiding a cache:

1. Scout a location and find a good hiding spot there, along with permission to use it.

2. Pull together an appropriate container and goodies, including a log book, to fill it.

3. Hide the cache in its new home.

4. Post the cache on one of the geocaching Web sites.

5. Follow up on any e-mail comments or questions from people trying to find the cache.

6. Periodically check the cache's condition.

Remember that you are doing a service to all of geocaching every time you place a cache: someone can hunt a cache only if someone else has hidden it. So let's find the hiding place.

Scout a Location

In all professional sports, teams employ scouts to search high and low for promising talent to fill the future ranks. This is necessary because fans aren't willing to watch personal attendants wheeling cadres of well-paid geriatric contenders across the old home field.

Geocaching is different, in that the participants can be of any age. Instead of constantly changing the players, you must constantly change the playing ground, and it is location that constrains all other things: cache type, access, difficulty, and clues.

Finding an Area with Potential

Gathering a list of potential cache spots is actually easier than deciding on a single one. Good locations are virtually everywhere you look, if you gaze with the right frame of mind. It's best to start considering hiding a cache after you have some seeking experience under your belt—maybe 10 to 15 caches. At that point, you begin to get a sense of what a cache hunter would view as a problem or an appreciated challenge.

There are two good ways of finding potential cache spots. One is to keep your eyes open and see potential areas around you. Here are some potential sources:

- Parks

- Nature reserves

- State forests

- Town public land

- Federal lands open to the public

One of your criteria can be (and in my estimation should be) the intrinsic interest of the location arising from such factors as aesthetic beauty, cultural significance, or historic importance, like the view from one of my caches as shown in Figure 7-1.

There are many places—hidden gems—that lack the public appreciation they deserve. I've seen caches hidden out in the sticks, in suburbs, and in the middle of a city. You can also keep your eyes open by keeping your ears open, because someone may mention an area that sounds appealing. Guide books of your home area are fair tools to use, too.

The other main way of choosing a place is to rifle through your memory for potential spots. Remember that because you know a place, others may not, or might not have been there in some time. In any case, check to see what you are allowed to do.

Figure 7-1 Out-of-the-way view behind a cache location

Getting Permission

A few caches do sit on private property—either that of the cache owner or someone else who is allowing cachers to search—but the vast majority are hidden on public land. Those are the sites that offer the greatest variety and natural beauty or historic interest.

Anyone who has grown to understand the difference between *mine* and *yours* knows why a cacher would need permission before placing a container on someone's property. Some types of land fall somewhere between public and private. Many conservation groups, ranging from the Audubon Society to state nonprofit organizations, own land that they make available for public enjoyment; this is not a right to do as you will without permission. Luckily, a good number of these groups are willing to cooperate if cachers will ask first and follow any restrictions or guidelines.

But even with public property, it is important to talk to the organization responsible for the land. It has a mission, incorporated into its creation, that the employees must uphold as best they can. This may include keeping the grounds so that the public may enjoy them, or it may include preventing too many people from entering a wilderness area that is a wildlife refuge.

To some, like the people responsible for the U.S. National Park system, planting any type of cache is akin to leaving trash in an area, because its very presence interferes with the natural order of things. This is an extreme view and, happily, one different from that held by most organizations. The Bureau of Land Management and the U.S. Forest Service both permit geocaching on lands open for general public use. Many state and local park and forest services have welcomed geocachers, who generally are an ecologically sensitive and cooperative lot who help bring locations to wider attention.

> **NOTE** At the time of my writing this, the Parks Advisory Commission in Ann Arbor, Michigan, had passed a resolution requiring people to obtain a permit before locating geocaches in city parks. There may come a day that you are required to obtain permission, rather than exercise reasonable care and thoughtfulness. And when permits exist, one must wonder: can user fees be far behind.

But even with groups that might tolerate a cache, it is important to ask before planting one. One reason is simple: if officials don't know what a cache is, they might indeed think it is trash and simply throw it away without looking inside. This has become particularly true since the question of terrorism has made many people hypersensitive to unrecognized containers showing up in unusual places.

Those officials can also provide crucial information and suggestions that can make your cache more successful. It might be that the old log you've eyed for an easy find just off the trail was scheduled for removal the day after you would have planted a container. Those in charge of an area can offer insight into the history or local flora and fauna that might enrich the experience of those on the hunt. They can inform you of potential seasonal problems in one area or another, such as high water from melting snow in the spring or particularly vigorous poison ivy coverage.

Such information is only useful when you consider it in relation to the type of cache you would set up.

Choosing the Cache Type

Tied intrinsically to the location is the cache type. Remember that there are different types of caches, and some work better in particular environments than others. Urban settings are usually best matched to a micro, or at least a small, cache. Hiding places large enough for a more generous cache are few and far between, though there are some. For example, check the now sadly archived Cache Me If You Can cache on Geocaching.com, as shown in Figure 7-2. It was a full-sized cache hidden in the heart of Boston that I had the pleasure of doing with my family.

Other cache types have their requirements. A multi-cache works best when there is a good reason for someone to move from place to place, like caches that move you from a forest area to a water view. There should be a variety of scenery, and enough plain old room to put some distance between the cache stages. In fact, if you are going to place a traditional cache in a large area, it's polite to try to place it in such a way that it does not interfere with other caches. (More on this later in the chapter.) A traditional cache is more flexible, though, and can work in a relatively small area.

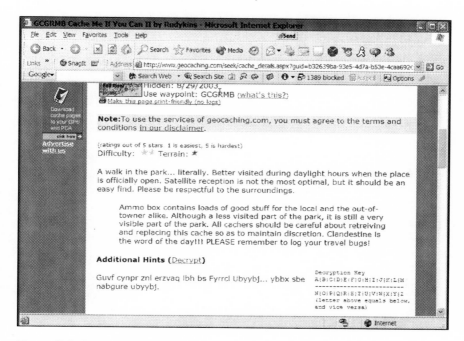

Figure 7-2 Cache Me If You Can

Some places rule out entire categories of caches. The National Park Service does not allow people to leave anything, including caches, behind them after a trip. That means no traditional caches, no multis, not even micros; you are limited to virtual caches, where people prove that they have been there either by taking a photograph, usually showing someone holding a GPS unit up, or by providing to the cache owner information available only to a visitor. However, a place that has reasonable hiding places is much better treated as a regular cache, because there are many people who don't like virtual caches.

Hiding a cache is only fun if someone will eventually come look for it, so part of finding a good location is choosing one that will be appealing. Remember that you have to rate the difficulty of the hunt as well as that of the terrain. The more difficult the experience, the fewer people who will try it. As the rates creep up over 2.5 or 3, the number of attempts to find it will dramatically drop. That is not to say that all caches should be relatively simple; in addition to the easy "drive-up" variety, there is room for the hard-to-reach searches that involve scuba, rock climbing, kayaking, or challenging hikes, and the difficult ones requiring advanced mental agility. Just realize that much of the fun in hiding caches is seeing others find them and post their results. The single largest factor in the rating of the entire cache is the hiding place.

Picking the Hiding Place

You may have the general location, but that is still short of choosing the actual hiding place, and things now get picky. There are a number of concerns you must balance:

- Cache type and potential spots
- Difficulty and terrain
- Safety
- Environment

Creating a good caching experience is a matter of trading off one consideration against another to find a happy medium.

Cache Type and Potential Spots

The nature of the cache and its size will dictate where you can hide it. The bigger the container, the fewer places you will find large enough to conceal it. A micro cache, on the other hand, could appear in any of the spots that would hold a good-sized container and quite a few others in addition.

Experienced cachers will usually check certain types of places: hollow logs, spaces underneath a log or rock, or spots next to trees that would be invisible from the trail, like the ones in Figure 7-3.

But there is little limit to what can serve as a hiding place. The crook of a split tree, if not particularly visible to people walking by, might cradle a container. A piece of pipe needn't be cavernously wide to accept a 35mm film canister.

> **NOTE** There is a literal ground rule: don't bury the cache. As no cache hiding spot is universally obvious (why bother to look, otherwise?), you could comfortably wager that people would start digging in the wrong spot. The only time this is generally considered acceptable in caching circles is if you bury a container in sand near the beach, so there is little chance of disturbance affecting the pleasure of others or tipping other geocachers to the location of the cache.

The quest for hiding spots can take a devious turn. Some cache owners have used hollow fake rocks and put them among their more genuine namesakes. Several people have taken dead tree stumps, sawn off the top, hollowed the center, then replaced the top and situated what was now a container into an area. In these cases, the hiding places *are* the caches. Others have hoisted containers overhead among trees or glued magnets to micro containers and stuck them to some out-of-sight steel surface.

Deftly concealing a container's true nature can greatly increase a spot's ability to hide a cache. Some people paint their cache containers with camouflage colors to better blend into the natural background, and others have gone so far as to glue leaves to the exterior.

I've seen at least one container simply covered with stray branches and pieces of bark so that it lay unnoticed on the ground less than ten feet off the trail.

Figure 7-3 Examples of cache hiding spots

Virtual and webcam caches have different considerations. The point of a virtual is to have people prove that they were at the spot. If you decide to require finders to e-mail corroboration, then try to pick a number or words or some bit of information that can only be found at the site. Try searching the

Web to see if you can find what you are requesting; should you locate it, choose something else less readily available to those who are seeking from an armchair. Requesting a photo with someone's GPS in it can eliminate the chance that people will take an old vacation picture or some image from the Web to fake the find. Remember, however, that not everyone has a digital camera or scanner, so you might want an alternative for the image-challenged.

With a webcam cache, you actually need to go to the Web to pick the camera first. Check that site to see when the camera is on, how often the image refreshes, and whether the camera moves position. Print a picture of the image and take it with you. Examine the area on foot and be certain that people can position themselves in the correct place.

But virtual caches are the exception, because there are many more of the traditional type. The way you hide a container has a direct bearing on the cache's difficulty—one of the two types of ratings you must assign to your cache.

Difficulty and Terrain Ratings

Every cache presents some degree of challenge to the finder, reflected in the 1-to-5 rating used for both the difficulty and the terrain. The combination approach works well, because it lets someone separately assess the qualities of the looking and the getting there. Half steps of rating (e.g., you could have a cache with a difficulty of 2.5 and terrain of 1.5) offer additional discrimination.

Part of the challenge is out of your hands; some people are better at finding caches than others, and there are those who will scamper up slopes that would leave others huffing and puffing. There are times when the ease of finding a cache has a direct relationship to the person's state of mind. I remember searching for a cache after a winter storm. One of the most experienced cachers in my area, who had many hundreds of cache finds, had preceded me there and I could still see his footprints in the snow. As I later learned, he searched for an extended time but found nothing, even after requesting a hint from the owner. I followed his steps for a bit, then decided to start looking in areas where he hadn't stopped. Sure enough, I was able to find the cache. Was I a better cache seeker? No. But for whatever reason, he was having a difficult time caching that day.

On a multi I had placed, two geocachers with more than a thousand finds between them e-mailed me because they could not find the second stage. I went out to meet them; lo and behold, that intermediate cache—a metal capsule about half-an-inch long and a quarter-inch wide—was not where I had left it. It had gone missing—maybe knocked loose by someone or something, but certainly not in site—and I had to replace it. (Who said it should be easy?)

The fault was mine, because I had wrapped the small item in a plastic bag and buried it under some leaves. However, it would have been easy to accidentally brush the container off into the distance while searching. I sent them on their way and put a replacement capsule in a more secure spot where it would likely withstand future reckless scrutiny.

Errant conditions aside, most of the difficulty in finding caches has to do with how well the container is hidden (assuming that you have accurate coordinates). This is a good point to again mention that the more difficult the cache, the fewer the people who will look for it. Looking at the 1-to-5 rating scheme, consensus has it that a difficulty of 3 begins the realm of "no-cachers land." Table 7-1 gives you some rules of thumb, available in an automated Web rating engine designed by cacher Clayjar and available at **www.clayjar.com/gcrs/**.

Table 7-1 Difficulty Ratings

Difficulty Rating	Conditions	Expected Time to Find
1	You can either see the cache or it is lightly covered.	You should find it within 15 minutes or so.
2	The cache sits happily well hidden and will require diligence, or there are multiple potential hiding places, or there is more than one stage.	It could take a half hour to an hour.
3	The cache is well hidden and there are a dozen places it could be, or this is a multi where each stage will require some diligent searching.	If you don't get lucky, you could conceivably spend a couple hours searching.
4	The cache is ingeniously hidden in a place where there are at least dozens of potential hiding spots, and is likely the last leg of a multi cache.	Most of a day or possibly multiple trips.
5	You will either need to recruit a member of MENSA to solve tough puzzles, or it is hidden in an extremely sneaky manner (hollow artificial rocks fall into this category).	Plan on the entire day or longer and read up on overnight camping.

Similarly, you must consider how to rate the terrain not just of the hiding place, but of the hike that cache seekers will cover to reach it. Table 7-2, representing the information available in an automated format at Clayjar's site, has some suggested ways to think of the terrain ratings.

Table 7-2 Terrain Ratings

Terrain	Explanation
1	Less than a half-mile hike on pretty flat ground, this will be an easy walk. It should be handicapped accessible, though not everyone will take that into account.
2	Still good for kids, the hike is under two miles on a marked trail, and any elevation changes are gradual.
3	You will be off-trail or on steep ground or hiking more than two miles; leave the kids at home.
4	Elevation changes may need some hand and foot climbing; you could be off trail and possibly hiking upwards of five miles or even more. This may require an overnight stay.
5	You are facing conditions demanding training, such as scuba diving, technical rock climbing, or kayaking, and you'll need specialized equipment, or the hike is going to be one of those stories you recite until people beg you to stop.

In other words, a caching outing can be anything from the literal walk in the park to an all-out amphibious assault. Also remember that ratings are intended for the most complicated part of the cache. If the terrain is mostly flat except for the last 30 feet, as happened to one cacher who told me of skidding down a sharp drop-off then having to climb back up, let the rating reflect the hardest part. A multi should be rated at least as high as the difficulty of any one stage, and preferably a half to a full point higher to indicate that there is even more to it.

No matter what the terrain and difficulty ratings, though, safety is an issue.

Safety

Geocaching is supposed to be fun and maybe aggravating on occasion, but never painful. Notice that I have not mentioned danger, because that is a relative concept. For example, after receiving my scuba certification, I had been trained in how to dive, with a buddy, under certain conditions. I've been as far as 90 feet underwater and gone drift diving at night. I could, and probably will, pursue some of the scuba-related caches, and likely plant one of my own. Someone without training could easily die in as little as 10 feet or 3 meters of water. However, if I were to set my sites on a cache that requires rappelling down the side of a cliff, I would advisedly make my hospital room reservation first. That is because I don't know the first thing about rock climbing. At the same time, training is relative, and there are scuba caches at depths and conditions beyond my training; blithely chasing after them would be foolhardy.

If you have created a difficult cache and safety demands special training or equipment, you had better make that crystal clear in writing in the beginning of the cache description. Yes, adults must make their own decisions about what they will or will not do—otherwise, the annual Darwin Awards, given to people whose monumentally foolhardy behavior leads to their early demise, would have little fodder. But there is no excuse for luring someone into starting a cache that they are ill-equipped to undertake. Even people who are trained and capable of going after a very difficult cache must know to bring the appropriate equipment with them; anything less is insulting and a waste of their time. Remember the golden rule in its everyday guise of common decency.

Safety doesn't begin and end with the massively difficult caches; you must consider it in every placement. Although not life threatening for most people, a brush with poison ivy, oak, or sumac is nasty. Searchers, like any people enjoying the outdoors, should know the signs of the plants, yet if a cache is hidden in a thatch of the plants, avoiding it might require abandoning the hunt. So the owners must be aware of their caches' settings. If placing containers in cold weather, then conversations with the operating authorities can be valuable, because they can explain the extent of problems posed. If there are any irritating plants, for heaven's sake mention it in the cache description: forewarned is forearmed . . . and gloved.

Are walking surfaces slick in wet weather, or at high tides or in storms? Mention that. Does approaching the cache require reaching over the edge of a cliff or even high rock? Say so. Climbing might require proper shoes; heavy mosquito infestation will need repellant. You may not be able to anticipate everything, but it doesn't hurt to try. Some consideration and planning can also go a long way in making caches friendly to the environment.

Ecological Concerns

Aside form the pleasure of solving problems and the interest in technology, the main reason for geocaching is to enjoy the outdoors. If done thoughtlessly, though, geocaching could harm the environment, and lessen the pleasure others may find.

Caring for the areas in which you and others travel is the responsibility that must be part of geocaching. A good deal of the duty lies with you when you place a cache. An ecologically sound choice can reduce wear and tear on the land and preserve habitats for wildlife.

Some people denounce geocaching, saying that it will inevitably lead to the destruction of whatever areas it touches. That is errant nonsense. The same logic might as well keep us all in our houses, never venturing onto green grass or crystalline ice, never seeing a robin close enough to count the feathers, never sitting on a rock, watching water bubble past. This book's technical editor has heard it called "the Dartmoor effect": if geocaching were going to trash the entirety of the outdoors, then letterboxing would have left Dartmoor National Park in England barren with the thousands of letterboxes that have been there over the years.

But as with most criticisms, there is a kernel of truth, because poor placement of a cache can cause long-term damage by directing people into treading overly sensitive areas, creating unnecessary trails, and unknowingly interfering with wildlife.

The first step of ecological respect is to ask the local authorities whether there are any considerations you should make when placing your cache. They will know of any conditions specific to the area. There are also general principles to acknowledge. If an ecologically sensitive area is near a cache, clearly make this point in the description, and tell people exactly where not to go. Trails being worn in areas deemed sensitive is what prompted Ann Arbor, so authorities say, to at least consider requiring permits. But damage could be done by anyone going off trail, including hikers, runners, and orienteering enthusiasts, even if caching is the easiest activity to blame because it relies on people looking for specific locations and Web sites can draw attention to what would otherwise be an invisible activity. Even though it may not seem fair, geocachers must walk the extra mile, so to speak, in considering the environmental impact of their activities.

Aside from the specifics of a particular area, you should keep in mind some general principles. For example, above the tree line (the elevation above which trees do not grow), plant life would be said to hang on to existence by its fingernails, if it had them. If you are going to place a cache in a high area, then find a spot that won't tempt someone to cross a fragile patch of growth. Avoid damaging or altering anything at your hiding site, such as hollowing an existing tree stump for concealment. (Bringing in your own, as some wily cache owners do, is different.) Some experts even suggest avoiding tree hollows that collect water, because small animals use them as a drinking source.

Deciding whether to hide a cache off-trail and by how far does become a topic that fires different opinions. One says that you should keep caches near trails to avoid creating new trails. Another says that caches should have some challenge, and putting them too near a trail makes detection by those not involved with geocaching more likely, so they should be placed far off the trail to make it less likely that people will follow the same path that creates a new trail. A third says that hiding something near a trail gets people to broaden the trail, bringing some sort of accompanying doom.

I must say that the considerations pro and con are prodigious and confusing. The theory is that if each person went off stumbling about as they would, then half of any given wild area would be trammeled in a thrice. So the best thing to do is take a step back and consider combining common sense with the leave-no-trace backpacking ethos, in which your passage through the outdoors should leave it as it was.

Certainly you can make things clear, as always, in the cache description. If someone needs to go off trail, say so; similarly, if a cache is near the trail, let someone know. Don't encourage unnecessary mulling about: there will surely be enough perplexity in finding the cache as to make blind trashing unnecessary.

If you want to place a cache off-trail, then look for areas that might allow travel using the leave-no-trace approach, as explained at www.lnt.org. Heavy forest area with little to no grass cover offers a firm surface that will remain largely undisturbed. If the ground is heavily overgrown with plants, then you might best serve all concerned to choose another spot. You must have searchers tread wearily in alpine reaches, though a local state forest might be reasonably clear and allow undamaging walking.

A highly sensitive area might be best for a virtual cache. Even though the choice of hiding place has an enormous determination of the ecologic impact, the particular container you pick also has an effect.

Assembling the Cache

You have many choices of container for a cache. Some basic characteristics you will want: either waterproof or highly water resistant, capable of undergoing the temperature extremes of where it will sit, and a resistance to damage.

Choosing a Container

For traditional caches, as Chapter 2 mentions, there seems to be yet another of these dual-camp approaches. One side likes the ammo can, a metal box that latches shut and is waterproof, while the other prefers the kitchen plastic container.

Ammo cans are generally metal containers, often found at military surplus outlets, meant to keep ammunition dry for use. Those who use them say that they could literally float in water. Because they are metal, they resist cold and heat, and they are also relatively easy to paint. But there is a problem. In days of concern about terrorism and danger, ammo cans are the sort of thing that could raise an alarm. That is the theory, at least; I haven't heard of a single case of an alarm raised about a found ammo can.

You can find plastic ammo cans and even plastic military "decon" boxes (used to hold decontamination kits—don't worry, they are safe). If you feel uneasy with the bellicose ambience, then you might appreciate the kitchen plastic container. Go for one of the sturdy types from such companies as Rubbermaid or Tupperware. I write a food review column, for which I've tested a number of the less commonly found types. If you run across the Snapware brand, snap it up—I've seen them keep an open bag of potato chips crisp for weeks. Although some people use them, I would avoid the disposable types of plastic containers. The material is thin and much more likely to suffer damage than the others. You save a bit at first, but may find it more trouble in the long run. Depending on the size, for extra protection you can always place the container inside a large plastic food storage bag with one of those zipping seals. The gallon freezer sizes are usually adequate for moderate-sized containers.

For smaller caches, a new world of containers becomes possible. Micro caches can use almost anything. Small metal tins (like the Altoids mint boxes) and plastic 35mm film canisters are popular, but not the be-all and end-all. I've even used a metal capsule—about .75 inches long and .25 inches in diameter—as the intermediate stages of a multi. A small slip of paper rolled up within gives you either the room to write the coordinates of the next stage, or some information or a message that someone must report back to gain credit for the find. (I wrapped the entire capsule in a plastic zipper-type bag for protection against moisture.)

But don't stop there: why not mark coordinates or a message on a card and waterproof it, or etch the information into a rock? I've seen caches where a foreign coin was cemented to a magnet, and the package stuck to a metal fixture; the finder would then provide the year and country of origin to the owner for the credit (Geocaching.com no longer allows that type, and requires every physical cache to have a logbook, though Navicache.com seems more flexible). The smaller the cache, though, the less room there is for the contents you might want to include.

Cache Contents

Micro caches show that you need not have a cornucopia of contents within the cache to make it effective. That aside, many people enjoy the process of a traditional cache, including trading things and filling out a log book.

Choosing the exact items is a matter of allowing your personal taste and interests to intersect with the size of the cache. I like to include a log book whenever possible, because it allows me to see if people really have been to the spot or are just trying to gain a credit. (Right: claiming a baseless find makes no sense, there is no advantage to be gained other than ego gratification, but since when did common sense direct human action?) More importantly, the log becomes a tangible memento of all that happened with the cache. Geocaching.com now has a minimum requirement for any cache container to contain a log. As the cache gets smaller, you may have to put together your own log book instead of buying a small notebook. I usually include a pen, though many people leave a pencil with a small sharpener; it has the advantage of never clogging in cold weather or running out of ink without warning. If your cache is small, check around for *golf pencils*, which are the tiny variety you receive with a score card at bowling alleys and miniature golf courses. They are available with an eraser, too. You can always go bowl a couple of frames or take in a round of putting before setting up your cache.

If there is enough room, place the log and writing implement in a large plastic bag within the cache. This serves two functions; it provides additional assurance of being dry, and it segregates the items so cache finders do not think these are subjects of a potential trade. Many people purchase a disposable camera and place it into the same bag. Those finding the cache then take a picture of themselves (long arms help); after finding that the film roll is finished, the owner has it developed and then often posts the images on a personal geocaching Web site or on the cache page.

A wise addition is the generic geocaching note. This is a sheet—sometimes placed within the log bag, sometimes laminated and separately added—that explains the concept of geocaching, asks that the cache not be disturbed by those stumbling upon it, invites the casual finder to join in the fun, and adds an offer to move the cache should its location be a problem. Geocaching.com has examples available for downloading, and they can be useful, but I prefer to create my own for a number of reasons. It's my cache and I want my personality to come through, for better or worse. I usually register my caches with both Geocaching.com and Navicache.com and don't want a bias toward one or the other. I also add an e-mail address if someone needs to reach me, rather than asking people to search through one of the geocaching Web pages: the easier they can reach me, the more likely they will and not just dump a cache.

Next come the goodies. There is no general way of choosing them. I usually create a theme for my caches and leave items that match, asking other people to do the same. For example, in the Reportage cache, which uses a theme of reporting, I left pens and reporter-style notebooks for the first half-dozen people to find it. I've seen or heard of caches with themes ranging from compasses to barnyard animals. Or you can forget the theme and leave any collection of items that strikes your fancy.

> **NOTE** *McToy* is a term (whether of toleration or derision depends on the user) for those disposable children's favors given out at fast-food restaurants. The argument against leaving them is their ubiquitous nature; everyone has seen them, and using them is just too easy. But some McToys have favorable characteristics—their small size makes them suitable for many caches, and some can be amusing. My compromise is to leave the McToys to my kids when they join me.

I've seen an amazing array of items, from gel pens and foreign coins, to a GPSr cover and music CDs. The effect of surprise and potential delight should be your guide. A good initial selection of cache items takes thought and some planning. As with the log, you might find it helpful for long-run maintenance to put them into a second large plastic bag.

You needn't break into the piggy bank to pay for a cache; in the United States, $10 to $15 should be enough for a container and some assortment of items to start. I can't vouch for prices in other countries. I tend to shop at high-discount stores with an eclectic collection of paraphernalia. There is one type of item that will cost exactly a dollar, and that is a Where's George? dollar. The site www.wheresgeorge.com allows people to register the serial numbers of dollar bills and then see how they move from one place to the next as finders spend them. Generally, the person who starts one in circulation writes the URL on the edge of the bill (as far as I know, it's legal). Some cachers are adamantly opposed to these dollars because they fear that when left in a cache, someone is likely to move the bill to yet another cache and not put it into circulation. They have a point, because the whole idea is to see how a bill travels when actually used, so go spend that money. Those of you who find such dollars (or other denominations and currencies that the site supports) and don't believe they should ever be cache fare are welcome to stick to principle and send the cash to me.

Mementos

Some people like to include items that will remind people of their caches. You can get a number of items specially made for geocaching that offer some personal twist or reference. One example is the cachecard, a little card that includes a picture of a site along with the name of the cache and its coordinates. You can find them at such sites as `www.cachecards.com` or `www.fredraab.com/cachecards/`, or could probably use the service of a business card printer who offers the inexpensive business cards sporting a photograph. Leave a supply of cards that people can take, and replenish them as necessary.

You can also leave your cachecards at caches you find, which will encourage others to visits yours. Some people have pins or buttons made with the cache's name. Another choice for a memento, mentioned in Chapter 2, is a geocoin.

Some cachers have geocoins made for them. Metal is certainly an attractive option, but wood is cheaper. You can search on the Web for custom coins (adding metal or wood as you want), and you'll see that metal versions run two to three dollars each in quantity, whereas the wooden ones might run 50 cents. Like travel bugs, some of these items have serial numbers, allowing them to be tracked from cache to cache. Check Appendix A at the end of this book for some geocaching-related sources.

Items on the Move

A new cache can be the springboard for items that you can follow from place to place. Hitchhikers, the serialized versions of geocoins, and travel bugs all offer ways of connecting your cache to others. Not only is it interesting and enjoyable to follow your object from one place to another, but you may find that every person who has helped it make geographic progress might also want to keep watch.

If you don't use travel bugs or serialized geocoins with their associated tracking mechanism, be sure to have a Web page devoted to keeping tabs on your moving mementos. If you can't set up forms that allow automated updates, then have people e-mail progress reports (noting the cache where the item was found and the cache where it was left) to you so you can post the information for everyone to see.

Now that you have your cache packed up and ready to place, it's time to hide it.

Hiding the Cache

Grab everything you need for the cache, including the container (packed and ready to go), secondary caches for a multi, and any camouflage materials you must bring, and drop them into your caching bag before heading to the site. You don't want to start by unintentionally involving the uninvolved by drawing attention to your geocaching activities. There is plenty of time to parade your pride and joy to the open air.

Also bring everything you would need for a cache hunt, from hiking boots and water to flashlight, and especially your GPSr, a notebook, and a pen or pencil. Although you know exactly where the cache will go, you must still travel there and back again, and the process of setting up a new cache can take more time than you might realize. If you think anything special is needed (there are some caches designed to be found only at night with a flashlight, for example), bring it and test the setup. Don't leave some unsuspecting cacher to be your guinea p…uh, evaluator.

Once you have arrived near the caching location, keep an eye out for passersby. If you need to use some local material for cover—branches, loose pieces of bark, rocks—gather it and have it ready. Now place the cache and cover it.

You might think you are done, but au contraire; the most important step is to come. To have people try the cache, you must offer proper coordinates. The difficulty is that a GPSr's signals are not guaranteed to offer absolutely accurate coordinates. For proof, start your receiver, walk to a spot near your cache location, and check the GPSr. Go back the next day, and you'll find the numbers are different—maybe a bit, maybe a lot.

Giving people the more accurate coordinates requires that you capture the best coordinates you can. There are different schools of thought (by now you didn't think there would be just one) that actually depend on the model receiver you have. Some products from Magellan and Garmin have an averaging feature in which the receiver takes a number of readings and automatically averages them. People using less capable receivers can take a number of readings, then average all the results for the one they will use. Then there are those like me who take a more simplistic approach. A GPS receiver cannot guarantee perfect coordinates, and there is no saying that the average of a number of readings is necessarily going to offer an improvement in accuracy. So I make sure the GPSr is on for a good 10 minutes beforehand, and when I've hidden the cache, I place the receiver near and wait for a few minutes before taking the coordinates. That allows the readings to come to some semblance of decisiveness. Be sure, however, when you are ready to provide those numbers for the cache listing, that the receiver is set to use WGS84 coordinates, unless you have an unrepentantly cruel streak and want to provide numbers that will leave people lost and angry. (If you export the coordinates though EasyGPS or one of the other Topografix products, the translation happens automatically.) Once you have the coordinates, it's time to tell other people about the cache.

Posting the Cache

You must let people know about your cache somehow. For public caches, and to be available to the greatest number of people looking for a cache, you should head to the geocaching Web sites to let the world know about your new hide.

> **NOTE** Many people post caches only on Geocaching.com. It certainly is the place to find the greatest number of active cachers, and I do tend to check there more regularly, but on general principles, I also tend to post caches on Navicache.com. In my view, geocaching needs a broad base of activity, so posting on all the sites can only improve things overall.

You must prepare certain types of information about your cache for any of the Web sites:

- Name: A cache by any other name would be another cache. This helps cachers keep their finds straight. You can choose anything as a basis for the name: location, cache theme, a historic reference, nod to a local legend, or just whim. Puns can be fun. Be creative.

- Coordinates: You got them with your GPSr when you planted the cache. All the sites use the WGS84 datum, so you must too.

- Size and type: Tell people the type of cache (multi, traditional, micro, virtual, locationless) and, if there is a container to find, its rough size.

- Date placed: That should be the date you put the cache in place, not the date that you filled out the form.

- Location: Be ready to offer a city or town, state or province, and a country. You may have to provide a zip or other postal code, depending on the country. For most people, it is easier to use location than coordinates to plan a cache outing.

- Difficulty and terrain ratings: You provide the 1-to-5 ratings, in half-step increments, that you determined after hiding the cache.

- Short description: This is a succinct explanation of the cache and conditions, such as "An easy three-stage multi in an old forest." Try to give a sense of what the experience might be like.

- Long description: The longer description serves to convey all the information you must provide. This should include any required equipment and training for scuba, kayaking, rock climbing, or other specialized needs. If an area is open only during certain hours, or if it is popular and will have a large number of passersby, mention that here. Explain if there are multiple caches or if cache containers are unusual in size (film canister) or appearance (artificial rock). Some sites actually have check boxes for listing where there are bathrooms, parking, fees, snack bars, or facilities for pets. Explain any unusual conditions, such as slippery footing in wet weather or a placement that could be dangerous for young children. In short, tell people everything they need to know.

- Hints: There are times when any geocacher, no matter how experienced, has difficulty with a given cache. Hints are just that: information that helps people when they just can't find the damned thing. I prefer to make mine slightly cryptic so that seekers would have to think for a second, but the clue would make sense in context. Some cache owners will offer blatant clues, like "look under the large rock shaped like Greenland." In any case, each site has a way of automatically encrypting hints, leaving it to the seekers to either use the clues or not. Avoid providing bad or useless information—such as, "Cache is not painted blue"—unless you are looking to transform some weary seeker, who has labored unsuccessfully for an hour, into a gibbering idiot.

- Photos: Some people upload photos of a cache, which can be important if its form is unusual. Others offer an image of the surrounding area, or a hiding place for those who are having trouble finding it. If a photo will give away the location, label it a *spoiler*, the general Internet term for any information that gives away the end of something intended to challenge, puzzle, or surprise you.

Each site has its own mechanism and format for providing the cache information. The sites also differ in their standards for approving new hides. Just because you enter the cache information does not mean that the major geocaching sites will list it. Your cache may be judged to be too close to another, not descriptive enough if a virtual cache, or in violation of such policies as burying a cache or keeping caches off restricted areas like U.S. National Parks. I've had a cache that started with coordinates to a parking lot and continued with directions of how to find the cache: Geocaching.com posted it, but Navicache.com responded that they would post no cache in which the exact coordinates were not provided. From my personal experience, I've seen that trying to correspond with a site about a cache can be next to useless on the odd occasion. Other people have told me similar stories. Another cache was deemed "not descriptive enough" for a virtual. I became irritated, but eventually took what is my current advice to others: Don't let it bother you. You can always adjust the cache so that it will be accepted, or you can create a private cache.

In a private cache, you inform only a select group of its existence. This may be through a personal word or note to cachers in your area (more on caching groups in the next chapter) or an announcement on your own cache-related Web site. I've seen one clever method in which the critical information about the cache was attached to a hitchhiker that moved from one cache to another. Some people would follow the progress to see if they too could eventually find the private cache.

Regardless of whether you choose to make your cache public or private, all cache owners must follow the progress of their own caches.

Proper Cache Follow-Up

Cachers have a derogatory phrase: drive and drop. It refers to someone who goes to a place with little thought or planning and leaves a container, calling it a cache. The same term can apply to caches that are left without attention. Every cache needs follow-up. You should periodically visit your own caches; once every month or two seems a reasonable schedule. A physical visit lets you see that the container is intact; determine if you must replace a logbook, pen, plastic bag, or disposable camera; and know that the cache is actually still there.

Seeing the actual log book lets you check who actually visited the cache and who only claimed a visit. As the cache owner, you can decide if someone has fulfilled the conditions for claiming a cache or not. If someone hasn't, delete that log, and they will lose the credit.

> **NOTE** Some people have started a new cache by changing the description and name of an older one they had placed and deleting all the logs. This is bad form, because doing this erases the credit for all the seekers who had found it.

The need for follow-up is a good reason to place your caches near where you live and work, or in places to which you can regularly travel. If you start dropping caches while at a destination unusual for you, there will be no practical way for you to provide the proper attention. You may also be unfamiliar with any local land managers' guidelines for caching. One way around this problem is to partner with someone who can check the cache at times.

Aside from regular visits at different times of the year (to be sure that seasonal changes, such as foliage dropping away or snow covering the ground, don't render caches considerably harder or easier to find), pay attention to the logs posted on your cache pages (generally, you will receive copies by e-mail). A sudden run of people unable to find your cache may indicate a problem that you must rectify. This brings up a second type of follow-up: not with the cache itself, but with those who seek it. You will receive questions from people who cannot find your cache, and it is only polite and reasonable to answer them as quickly as is reasonably possible. Imagine the annoyance of being unable to find a cache and e-mailing the owner, looking for a hint, only to receive no response.

Checking the cache page logs also lets you monitor the experience people have with your cache. If you rank the difficulty as a 3 and you see multiple comments of how easy it was, you might think of lowering the difficulty rating. Something I've done after a cache has received a few visits is to look at the list of people who found it, check their experience in the number of caches they've found, and ask the more experienced seekers if the rating seemed fair to them. On any of the geocaching sites, you can edit the cache descriptions, including the difficulty and terrain ratings, at any time. Use feedback wisely and adjust as necessary. Remember, too, that seasonal variations can warrant rating changes; a 1 difficulty may become a 5 with two feet of snow on the ground.

Now that you can hunt caches and place your own, it's time to consider some of the variations beginning to appear in the sport, as the next chapter discusses.

Geovariations

"No pleasure endures unseasoned by variety."—Publius Syrus

Some people can live with sameness. Most, on the contrary, need change to their schedules, surroundings, activities, and even weather. Similarly, doing one easy cache after another can become boring. But there are ways of breaking up the sameness. One is to choose harder caches—even to the point of extreme geocaching. Another is to explore some of the related activities that can expand your enjoyment of geocaching.

You can expand your geo-centric borders in a number of ways. Here are some suggestions to get you started:

- Extreme geocaching

- Benchmark hunting

- Becoming a GPS tracker

- The Degree Confluence Project

- Other GPS games

- Geocaching in a crowd

- Geocaching on vacation

- Geocaching in education

And remember that this is a rapidly evolving activity invented on the whim of someone on an Internet newsgroup; there is no reason you cannot create your own variations.

Extreme Geocaching

I've mentioned this before, but there is geocaching, and then there is geo-caching. A cache hunt can be an easy walk through a gentle wood, but the fun can mount with the difficulty and terrain. Consider hiding and seeking caches that involve any of the following:

- Scuba diving and snorkeling

- Kayaking or boating

- Rock climbing

- Backpacking

- Extreme weather

- Night

All these variations take some preparation and even training, but the results will be worth the effort.

> ⚡ **CAUTION** Although challenging and fun, it would be the height of idiocy to try any of these without the proper training and experience. If you don't know what you are doing, some of these activities (I can talk from experience about scuba diving) can quickly land you in a hospital bed—or coffin.

Scuba Diving and Snorkeling

A few months before beginning this book, I had a writing assignment that involved learning to scuba dive, which fulfilled a long-held desire. It can be expensive, and requires significant preparation to go underwater even for 40 minutes to an hour, but don't let that stop you.

Finding caches hidden underwater can be tricky. For example, using the search term *scuba* on Geocaching.com's cache search page will turn up only a few listings with scuba in the title, so also try looking for *underwater*. (Or you can use the trick with Google.com that Chapter 6 mentions.) In comparison to traditional caches, only a handful exist, so you may find yourself doing more hiding than seeking. But any excuse to get underwater is a good one.

When creating a cache, indicate if a particular amount of scuba experience is necessary for the hunt. For example, a cache sitting 100 feet (30 meters) underwater is at a depth appropriate only for advanced open-water divers, but not those newly certified. If these terms aren't familiar, that is warning enough to steer clear. You can get dive training at many places. PADI, the Professional Association of Dive Instructors, is the largest association of dive instructors. I received training through a PADI-affiliated dive shop and found it clear and complete. There are other groups, such as NAUI and the YMCA, that also offer a full set of diving courses, and any should fit your needs. If you have a number of choices available, try interviewing the instructors to see if any seem a better fit with your inclinations and needs.

To allow divers to adequately assess the cache's requirements, be sure to indicate the depth of the cache in your description. Because a GPS unit will be useless under water, provide coordinates to the best departure point and then offer directions with compass bearings. Give plenty of clues and describe the appearance of the cache and where it might be found, because air supply and decompression considerations limit search time. If there are any special considerations, such as exceptionally turbulent tidal changes or limited visibility requiring a diver's flashlight, be sure to mention them.

The cache itself will take thought and planning. Some underwater caches use a negatively buoyant container (it sinks) filled with objects that can withstand exposure to water. In these cases, the diver brings a suitable item for trade, making the swap and any log notations (on waterproof paper, presumably) while submerged. Some caches have a weighted container anchored to some item underwater, but require the finder to bring it to the surface, because the contents are supposed to remain dry. In yet another variation, the owner establishes a multi and anchors a plaque or other object bearing the coordinates of the final container.

If you are going to hunt an underwater cache, pour through the description and first determine if your experience and training are enough to attempt the find. Look for any special equipment that you might need—a flashlight, or a slate for noting GPS coordinates for a final land-based cache. Pay close attention to the directions, and consider either copying them to your slate or encasing them in a waterproof carrier or lamination so you can refer to them while on the bottom. And no matter what, remember that the hunt is secondary to diving safety. Always dive with a buddy, mind your depth and time limits, and leave your plans with someone who expects a check-in call at a certain time.

Some underwater caches don't require scuba gear, but instead can be found by snorkeling. That does not eliminate the safety considerations; you still need a dive buddy and should have learned how to correctly and appropriately snorkel to avoid potential hazards like shallow-water blackout, in which people can fall unconscious while holding their breath with no warning of trouble. The two of you should take turns looking for the cache and accept that it's the team, not the individual, making the find.

Kayaking or Boating

Some caches located on islands require use of a boat. A kayak is a pleasurable and active choice, as is a canoe; a motorboat is considerably faster. Any watercraft requires three things: an understanding of safe and proper use, the skill required to operate the craft, and the actual craft itself.

Rental can take care of the third, but the first two considerations need, again, training and experience. From proper knot tying to paddling technique, engine safety, and maritime "rules of the road," this is not knowledge available simply from a book; learning must accompany doing. Techniques in one craft may not transition smoothly to another; for example, canoe paddling is different from kayak paddling. You can find training in a number of places. A local outdoor store may offer kayaking lessons, and a quick look on the Web will find many other outlets. For general boating safety and navigation, the Coast Guard's boating safety Web site (`www.uscgboating.org`) is a comprehensive resource.

If you establish a cache that requires a boat, be sure to provide any relevant information that the pilot will need. Are there docking restrictions at the destination? Is there a place to launch the boat and leave a car, and possibly a trailer, parked? Are any facilities open to public use? Carefully consider the placement of the cache, because you need a publicly accessible route from the landing point to the container. If there are ecologically sensitive areas that cachers should avoid, point this out to avoid damage. Also hesitate before deciding to place the cache so that it is available only from the boat itself. I've seen at least one disturbing story of someone footing a ladder in a boat before reaching up to the hiding place. If people are determined to be physically foolish, that is their right. But a cache should always be available to someone willing to take a safe, even if difficult, route.

If seeking a cache, check nautical charts for the area. Be sure that your approach to a landing spot has water deep enough for your boat. When you use a boat in caching, weather information becomes critical; a rain storm that makes caching difficult on land could mean a small-boat advisory is in effect, which should prohibit using water-borne craft. Bring an appropriate flotation device for each person going, as well as charts, your GPS, and a compass. And be sure to leave your plans and expected route with someone who will expect your call at a given time. Do not, for any reason, fail to make the call, and do not assume that your cell phone will work. Give yourself enough time to do the search and return to an area with viable reception.

Rock Climbing

Some cache owners like bringing you to the edge of a cliff, and others like to take you over. Rock climbing, like scuba diving, is an activity that can leave you hurt faster than you can say splint.

It should go without saying that when a cache warns those attempting it to be trained and equipped rock climbers, you should not reach for an old pair of sneakers and an old coil of rope that has been sitting about. You should bring full equipment and a partner to stay on belay (controlling the rope) at the top of the cliff. For training, check the Web and local outdoor stores; aside from kayak training, EMS in my area offers climbing courses at a nearby quarry.

Both owners and cache hunters alike should use reputable climbing guides for the areas in question. Climbs have standard difficulty ratings, and you don't want to be caught in a situation beyond your current capabilities. Some caches may not explicitly call for climbing equipment, but a rope might provide some welcome security. So for any cache that invokes the word *climb*, be sure to read the logs of previous visitors, because you will get a sense of what unstated precautions might be advisable. As always, leave your plans with people who can call the authorities if you do not make the safety call.

If you must use climbing equipment, be sure you have something to keep you suspended in midair next to a cliff so that your hands are unoccupied for the search. Caches placed into a rock face are usually going to be micros, because a small item will fit best into a crack. So realize that even if a trade is possible, it will be a small item. Check the description thoroughly and get a sense of the dimensional restrictions. A larger opening, on the other hand, might permit a standard-sized cache. If you are the owner, remember to think sturdy, because checking on the cache might be difficult, and you want something that can withstand prolonged time in the outdoors.

Backpacking

The occasional cache involves a long hike in to the container and back out again. When you see an extended distance, consider taking a backpacking trip, with an overnight stay providing the rest between the two legs of the journey.

You needn't look to paying an instructor to learn, as this really is an activity well suited to the application of book learning to boot leather. If you are an experienced backpacker, then use that knowledge, remembering to add to your pack the extras you need for geocaching. If inexperienced, travel with someone who has been "down the trail" before.

It has become standard advice to only backpack with someone else, and those who are sensible should probably follow that rule. To be honest, though, I have backpacked by myself (after leaving proper notification of my where-abouts) because I crave the solitude unavailable in an urban or even suburban region. Perhaps it's a personal blindness—I would certainly not go scuba diving without a buddy—but one that I cannot willingly suspend.

Backpacking is something that you can pick up to a far greater extent from books than scuba, boating, and climbing. If you have done little, read and think before you travel. Better to over-prepare than under-enjoy. The books listed in Appendix A offer some good sources of information.

Extreme Weather

Many geocachers wait for the best weather, looking for warm, sunny days. I am not one of them. I've gone in the rain, wind, sleet, snow, and heat. The obvious advice is to dress for the conditions in the cache area (Chapter 5 discusses this). Perhaps less obvious is that seemingly off-putting weather actually can be something to be savored. We have precious little time on this earth, and joy can encompass all that we can experience, if we accept its beauty. To walk though a fog breathing soft on the land's colors, to hear the rain percussion not on the roof but on your jacket, to feel the sun toasting your skin, they are all wonders. Why keep yourself separated from this sensation by merely peering at it from behind a window? Of course, there is extreme and then there is foolish, so sit out the hurricanes, tornados, and blizzards.

One type of weather can, however, have a devious effect on your activity: snow. A cache rated 1/1 can turn into a 4/4 or 5/5 with two feet of powder on the ground. In this circumstance, a stick used as a probe around will be a valuable asset. (Who says that a walking stick is good only for transportation?) Realize that the snow can make your search obvious to anyone passing, whether involved in geocaching or not. Try not to make your prowling obvious. That may include using a branch to brush out your footprints, or being reconciled to possibly going back for a second search.

Night

Some people call off caching at dusk; for others, this is the time to start look-ing. In fact, some caches are designed to be found only at night, usually calling for flashlights shining on reflective tape to pinpoint the container's location.

Caches become more difficult because there is less light for the looking, because things seem different, and because you may be more prone to trip-ping. I don't tend to cache at night, though I greatly enjoy hikes then. Here are a few pointers from my experience and passed on by devotees.

You obviously need to bring light. Instead of just flashlights (and they are a must), try a head-mounted lamp. I use a Black Diamond Moonlight model, which throws light 20- to 30-feet ahead by using LEDs that provide an easy glow with lower power consumption than conventional bulbs. Although there are cheaper models, I find the $30 well spent. Batteries mount at the back and the lamps on the front, with straps on the side and top of the head holding it all together. I've used lamps where the entire housing sat at the front with a single horizontal strap, and they tend to slide down unless strapped uncom-fortably tight. My lamp is easily comfortable for an hour or two at a stretch.

One cacher who often is out at night suggests filtering the lamp or building your own so the light is red, which preserves your night vision. If you need to turn it off for any reason, like trying to avoid being seen, you are less likely to be blinded by the dark. The principle sounds similar to a so-called safe light in a photographic dark room, where you must extinguish the light when exposing paper that will become a print, but where you need at least some dim reminder of where things are otherwise. To go this route, be sure to place a filter over the flashlight as well.

Because visibility is so limited, you need to take care. Before poking into dark places, shine in your flashlight and probe with a stick to be sure that you don't disturb some animal with sharp teeth and temper. Walking can also be trickier because of obscured footing. The headlamp will help immensely, but sometimes it is fun to walk in the dark, with only the moon and stars showing your way. At those times, lift your feet high when taking steps, and you will avoid many potential tripping hazards.

If extreme geocaching hasn't given you enough variety in your activity, then consider some of the other related activities you can pursue.

Benchmark Hunting

If you enjoy virtual caches at all and you are in the United States, consider benchmarking. Benchmarks are reference points left by survey teams: the National Geodetic Survey (NGS), the U.S. Army Corp of Engineers, the Bureau of Land Management, and various other state and local organizations. They show the location and sometimes height of known points, and allow land surveyors to make measurements that have a context. Benchmarks are small—a few inches across—and made of metal.

These benchmarks are usually out in the open, but are mostly ignored by passers-by. Some are set into the ground, some into manmade structures, some into natural features. Where, you might ask, is the challenge in looking for something well documented in plain view?

Edgar Allen Poe, the first author of detective stories, wrote *The Purloined Letter*, which pivoted on a letter hidden in plain sight; benchmarks can be much the same. Those who left them intended them to be easily found, but over the years, many have been lost, either destroyed, removed, or even forgotten. The NGS keeps a database of the benchmarks, and `Geocaching.com` has a benchmarking feature with a copy of that information. Using this feature, you can get approximate coordinates for benchmarks, along with descriptions of their settings. Many of these descriptions have been unchanged for years, even while things have changed around the benchmarks, so finding a benchmark can be harder than it sounds.

To find a benchmark, use the coordinates as a first approximation to its location. Then use the descriptions, trying to picture how things might have changed since.

When you do find a benchmark, you return to `Geocaching.com` and post your find. If possible, bring a digital camera and upload images of the benchmark and its surrounds. Under no circumstances should you take the benchmark, because it must remain in place for survey purposes. Contrary to what you might expect, many benchmarks sit on private property. Unlike with geocaches, there may be little indication if a benchmark sits on private land. So pay close attention: if you are about to step onto someone's property, ask permission or pass it up.

You could stumble across benchmarks that don't appear in the database, because so many different organizations have placed them. In that case, there is little to do, other than keep your own records, because the NGS database doesn't track all benchmarks, and `Geocaching.com` can do nothing with those not found in the database.

If tracking benchmarks does nothing for you, there are always other things, like tracking travel bugs, money, and books.

Becoming a GPS Tracker

Earlier chapters have talked some about tracking hitchhikers from one cache to another, and the special serial numbers available from Geocaching.com. It can be a pleasure and intriguing to see how things move from one place to the other, like Fishy, shown in Figure 8-1, that at the time of writing had traveled more than 1,710 miles in just over a year to meet his owner's first goal of arriving in San Antonio, TX, and then to continue visiting as many waterside caches as possible.

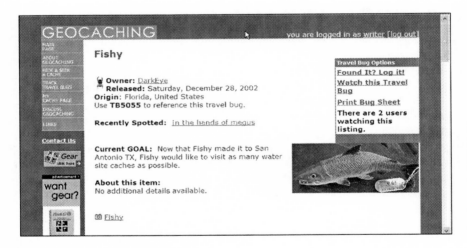

Figure 8-1 Fishy the travel bug

Furthermore, as Figure 8-2 demonstrates, you can click on the View Map button to see its current position.

In addition, if you click on the Old Map link, you can have a more expansive view of its travels, as shown in Figure 8-3.

> **NOTE** Don't get too attached to a travel bug, because *muggles* (a term, lifted by geocachers from the *Harry Potter* stories, meaning "the uninitiated") who come across a cache, or even ill-mannered cachers, can walk off with one. Even benevolent cachers can sometimes take a travel bug and neglect to move it along for a long period of time, if ever.

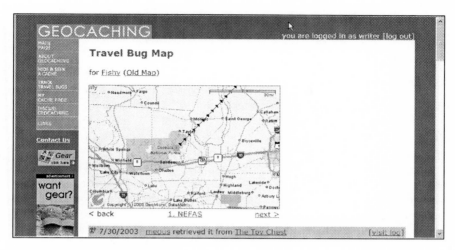

Figure 8-2 Fishy's travels

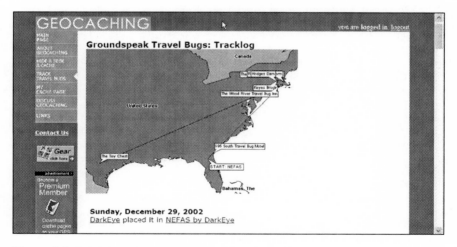

Figure 8-3 Fishy's long-distance travels

But travel bugs and hitchhikers are not the only things you can track. Various Web sites keep a watch on a number of things, including:

- Currency
- Books
- Journals

People run these sites as projects that can reveal how items typically passed from one person to the next might actually move through society.

Currency

Even though money may be a blessing or curse (depending on your perspective), it surely is fascinating. Forget economics macro and micro and think about cold, hard cash. Whether you live in Bangkok, Budapest, Brasília, or Boston, you are handling a local currency every day.

Ever wonder who had a bill before you, who might get it after, or how many miles it could travel in its life? The people at Where's George? (www.wheresgeorge.com) obviously had similar thoughts. Their site lets you enter the serial number of a bill, and thereafter you can obtain progress reports on the bill's movement, with such vital information as its last reported position and the number of miles it has traveled since the last update. By marking the edge of the bill with the URL, you can prompt others to also track its movement.

Where's George? only works for U.S. currency, but there are other choices, depending on your locale:

Canada: Run by the Where's George? owner, the Canadian version is Where's Willy?, predictably located at www.whereswilly.com.

Denmark: The Danes have "The Note," at www.sedlen.dk, and the krone, so celebrate variety.

Europe: EuroBillTracker, www.eurobilltracker.com, is for the ubiquitous European currency that to my mind has brought a visual dullness to the continent. Euro Swapper, www.euroswapper.net, focuses specifically on coins.

Germany: If you want to track Euros but speak German, try Wo ist Mein Geld? (or Where is My Money?) at www.woistmeingeld.de.

Japan: If you've traveled in Japan, then Osatsu.net (*osatsu* is Japanese for a bill), at www.osatsu.net, will let you fill your yen for tracking, or tracking your yen, with most of its pages also available in English.

Netherlands: The Dutch have Where's The Money, www.wheresthemoney.nl.

United Kingdom: Thank heavens that some countries can be in Europe but not of it. If you've been in the U.K., DoshTracker, www.doshtracker.co.uk, will let you put your money where your pound is.

If tracking money isn't to your taste, try books.

Books

Everyone knows the experience of lending books only to never see them again. Instead of bowing to the whims of bibliographic fate, take arms against a sea of borrowing and, by anticipating, end it.

At BookCrossing (`www.bookcrossing.com`), you can register a book that you've read, receive an identification number, and then label the book. Go someplace and simply leave the book for someone to take—or leave the book in a cache along with a note, instructing someone to read it and pass it along in a more conventional manner. Don't want to read what someone else wrote? Then do some writing.

Journals

The 1000 Journal Project is an experiment that is following a thousand paper journals through their travels. People write and draw and paste in photos in a section, then pass on the book to someone else. At `www.1000journals.com`, it's possible to sign up for a journal, though the site explains that the chance of your name coming up is virtually nil. However, you can search for journals by location and sometimes even see the e-mail of people who currently have them; with any luck, begging might do some good.

With the tracked currencies, books, and photographs, it's important not to allow the items to be tied up in a cache, but to keep them circulating. But there are other things to do with a GPS receiver and a taste for geocaching.

The Degree Confluence Project

If you love using degrees in coordinates, then the Degree Confluence Project might be appealing. Located at `www.confluence.org`, this is an attempt to document every intersection of whole number latitudes and longitudes. For example, 41°N 91°W is a spot in Iowa, and an example of whole number coordinates.

By going to the site, you can see the intersections by country and even by region, when the nation is physically large enough. After creating a free account, you choose a location and then file a plan to visit a particular confluence by using the form in Figure 8-4.

You specify the coordinates and also the date range during which the plan is in effect. If you complete and log your visit, along with the mandatory plethora of pictures, the plan cancels, as it's no longer needed. If you don't undertake the visit, then the plan times out on the last day. You can also request notification of anyone else's plans to visit a particular confluence, in case you are feeling competitive.

Speaking of competition, GPS provides many direct routes to it.

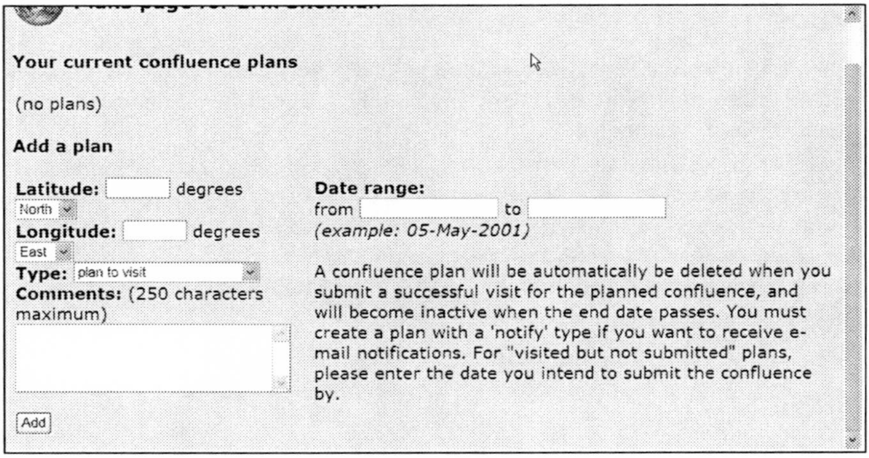

Figure 8-4 Filing a confluence plan

Other GPS Games

GPS receivers seem to lend themselves to all manner of geographically based activities. Garmin has at least one model with a number of built-in games, but you don't have to buy a particular model GPSr for these additional diversions:

- Geocaching Fox Hunt
- MinuteWar
- Geodashing
- Geodashing Golf
- GeoPoker
- Prize and competition geocaching

For some of these, you will need to recruit some help.

Geocaching Fox Hunt

This game, created by the Team Tate cachers in the United Kingdom, is based on an old amateur radio activity. Operators would seek a hidden transmitter by using radios and trying to zero in through various technical means.

In this version, the fox—the team that is being chased—travels about in a car with GPS equipment and a cache of goodies. The other teams—hounds—drive around trying to find the fox. The fox pauses at times to give hounds a chance to catch up. Hounds that find the fox get to swap items for those in the cache.

When played in the United Kingdom, a geocaching fox hunt has depended on the availability of a telematics device, which is a combination GPS receiver, mobile phone, and a user interface. It can generate SMS messages—a mobile phone feature in which you can send or receive brief strings of text—that contain the position and status of the telematics device. If it's in a car, that means the text messages can say where the car is, how fast it's driving, and in what direction.

The hounds drive around and send some pre-arranged code via SMS to the fox. In return, they get the fox's current coordinates, direction, and speed. This allows the hounds—best working in pairs, with one driving and the other navigating—to try to catch up and even anticipate the fox's future position.

Telematics units are expensive, and not all mobile phone services support SMS. In some other areas, like North America, you could be completely out of luck. But for those of us not on the technical leading edge, there is another solution: have a second person in the fox car sit with a cell phone and a GPS receiver. A member of each hound team can then phone and request the position information, using a map to plot direction.

Some cachers have considered other variations on a fox hunt that use a series of microcaches. The fox gets a head start and begins going to the caches, leaving some sort of token. Hounds go to a cache, collect the tokens, and return to a central point for coordinates to the next cache. I'm not clear on how someone catches the fox, or whether the idea is to do so. In a way, it doesn't matter, because this is an example of how you can take a geocaching idea and mold it to fit your circumstances and interests.

MinuteWar

Although not really a form of geocaching, MinuteWar is a version of capture the flag using GPS receivers. The concept is to visit specific locations and capture virtual flags, taking control of territory areas on a map. The winners are the people who hold the most land at the end of the game.

The clever trick of this game is to ignore the degree parts of positions and look at only the minutes (hence the *minute* part of the name). So, as the MinuteWar Web site (`www.minutewar.org`) explains, the following positions would be considered equivalent:

- N41° 51.749 W087° 36.967, which is in the United States

- N51° 51.749 W000° 36.967, which is in the United Kingdom

- S38° 51.749 E176° 36.967, which is in New Zealand

Furthermore, a player can specify an offset, or shift in the latitude and longitude, so that you can put your copy of the playing field in your backyard, more or less.

Games usually occur with two teams, split geographically into hemi-spheres, and a single game can run weeks. You need to sign up before a game starts and review the rules, as they can change from one to the next.

If you are interested, then visit the MinuteWar site and look at the practice session. This should help make the complexities clearer as well as giving you some practice while waiting for the next session of global warfare.

Geodashing

This is another GPS-related game (see `http://geodashing.gpsgames.org/`) cre-ated by the same person who brought you MinuteWar. At the beginning of a game, a computer chooses a large number of waypoints called *dashpoints*. The computer picks the locations at electronic whim, so the dashpoints may be on a city street or at the top of a mountain. The point of the game is to reach as many dashpoints as possible.

You can compete as an individual against other individuals, or you might enjoy working on a team competing against other teams. You must get within 100 meters (or about 330 feet) of as many points as possible and report the results to your team. Team members look at local maps, like the one of Western Europe in Figure 8-5, and pick dashpoints that they can reach, where each "+" is a dashpoint and a "V" is a dashpoint that someone has visited.

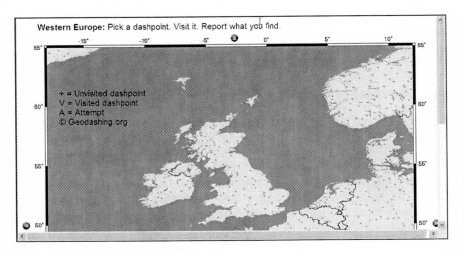

Figure 8-5 Geodashing map

This is a game that takes a full calendar month to run its course, which makes sense, because it takes time to plan those territorial assaults.

Geodashing Golf

Another variation of GPS games is a high-tech version of golf. In Geodashing Golf (`http://golf.gpsgames.org/`) the Web site assigns each player a set of 18 waypoints—the course holes. You get as close to each waypoint as you can. The closer you get, the lower your score on that "hole." Of course, there is no guarantee that the waypoint is going to be convenient or even within reach.

GeoPoker

Combining a card game with hiking—and some said that it couldn't be done. GeoPoker (`http://poker.gpsgames.org/`) is another of the games on the `GPSGames.org` site. It's a team game that involves players moving a container with a special log book. Every time one of the involved players finds the container, he or she gets to go to the site and receive a card. This continues until 52 cards are dealt, and whoever can make the best hand out of the cards dealt is the winner.

Prize and Competition Geocaching

Bitten by the treasure hunting bug, but looking for game bigger than McToys? The growing number of geocachers has caught the attention of the corporate marketing types, and they've been trying to use cache hunts in advertising campaigns.

When the remake of the *Planet of the Apes* was released, the studio started something that it nicknamed "Project A.P.E.," a series of caches hidden around the country. Recently, a well-known equestrian event, the Foxhall Cup, ran a geocaching event with prizes. A cacher in southern California has started a small-scaled game with prizes called Legendeo (`www.legendeo.org`), involving geocaching and puzzle solving. Entry fees are required if you want to win prize money, but you can play the game without it.

Some companies have tried to use geocaching as a marketing gimmick, having people search one way or another for prizes. More will probably come around, so just keep an eye open and take advantage of the opportunities when they present themselves to you.

One thing to remember is that geocaching is young, and there's room aplenty to have influence on the way things develop. If you feel inspired, invent your own variation. After all, that's all that everyone else has done so far.

Geocaching in a Crowd

You can multiply the geocaching fun by going with others. I've met cachers on the trail and have planned sessions with others. But there is a type of cache, at least on Geocaching.com, that I haven't mentioned before: the event cache.

This seems like any other cache, but with the difference that credit depends on being in a particular place at a particular time. An event cache is like a party where your GPSr is your invitation. Generally, those hosting the get-together plan some special caches, sometimes private ones available only for the gathering, and other times listed online and available to any cacher who goes to the area after. Sometimes they try entirely new variations on geo-caching, such as the fox hunts held in the United Kingdom or some combinations of geocaching and orienteering in the United States.

In some regions, people have actually created organizations of local cachers. Some are more active, others less, but all offer a chance to meet other participants, to learn, and to have fun. Literally dozens of organizations have been created around the world of regional geocaching groups, and Appendix A lists many.

Geocaching in Education

So far, the talk has been fun. But geocaching can serve a purpose in learning. Think of the concepts that geocaching involves:

Mathematics: From reading maps and understanding how to calculate distances between points to wrestling with the advanced coding concepts that allow receivers to calculate distances from satellites, GPS is steeped in mathematics.

Science: Geocaching relies on advanced communications science to make the concept of finding a position possible. Topics can include the nature of radio waves, compasses and the earth's magnetic field, and atomic clock theory.

Electronics: Advanced students can explore how to build receivers and antenna systems, or how to integrate GPS with computers.

Geography: Geocaching is a natural way of introducing maps and geography to students. They can learn to relate local geographic features to larger contexts, and can eventually study how geologic forces help shape the world as they see it.

Natural history: In geocaching, children come in contact with plants, trees, and ecological concerns. Teachers can naturally introduce botany and biology through direct observation and interaction.

Observation and logic: Young people trying geocaching must exercise discipline of the mind, from solving (or even devising) puzzles to developing an effective search strategy.

Students can then learn to apply all these disciplines in almost any setting, making geocaching a particularly rich educational experience. A growing number of teachers and students have taken an interest in geocaching. Some grade schoolers have already used it as a topic in science fairs, and a number of high schools have started geocaching clubs, getting teenagers out early on weekends and using their brains and bodies. Scouting is another area where geocaching is meeting youth; Camp Yawgoog, a scouting camp in Rhode Island, offers *geoscouting*, the hunting of treasures with a GPS unit. And other groups have begun to look at geocaching as a good activity for scouts.

Since its birth just a few years ago on the whim of someone's suggestion, geocaching has already come a long way. Whoever is involved can expect the road to be interesting—and fun.

Resources

Here are some print and online resources for all aspects of geocaching. I've grouped them by category so you can find what you seek more easily, or you can just browse. Sorry, but no waypoints for them:

Navigation covers all aspects of compasses, maps, and GPS.

Meeting the Outdoors provides general equipment resources and specialized activity resources.

Geocaching lists general and regional resources directly related to the activity.

Tracking Objects focuses on resources for keeping tabs on the worldly travels of inanimate objects.

Navigation

Compass

Cammenga (**www.cammenga.com**): Military style compasses.

Canadian Geomagnetic Reference Field (**www.geolab.nrcan.gc.ca/geomag/cgrf_e.shtml**): Find magnetic declination for areas in Canada with mathematical models designed for that country.

"How to Use a Compass" by Kjetil Kjernsmo (**www.learn-orienteering.org/old**): Illustrated guide to using a compass from an experienced orienteer.

National Geophysical Data Field (www.ngdc.noaa.gov/cgi-bin/seg/gmag/fldsnth1.pl): Find magnetic declination for any latitude and longitude.

How to Do It

Be Expert with Map and Compass: The Complete Orienteering Handbook by Bjorn Kjellstrom and Newt Heisley (John Wiley & Sons, 1994): One of the great books on using a compass, with an orienteering spin that won't do a bit of harm.

GPS Land Navigation: A Complete Guidebook for Backcountry Users of the Navstar Satellite System by Michael H. Ferguson (Glassford Publishing, 1997): A book about using GPS systems. There's a lot of good information, though the publication date was before the removal of selective availability, so some of the assumptions will be off.

How to Use a Compass (www.learn-orienteering.org): If you want to learn more about compass basics and don't want to buy a good book, point a browser to this site.

Land Navigation Handbook: The Sierra Club Guide to Map and Compass by William S. Kals (Sierra Club Books, 1983): More insights into using a map and compass to help find your way about.

Wilderness Navigation: Finding Your Way Using Map, Compass, Altimeter, and GPS by Bob Burns and Mike Burns (The Mountaineers Books, 1999): Another book that came out before the end of selective availability, but still a great title on navigation techniques, including some types of clues—like using elevation and slope—not found in other books I've read.

Maps and Aerial Photos

ChartTiff (www.charttiff.com): Electronic versions of topographic maps and aerial photos.

Geocode (www.geocode.com/modules.php?name=TestDrive_Eagle): Technology company site with test-drive feature allowing you to obtain coordinates from an address in the Unites States.

"How to Print Your Own Topo Maps" (`www.geocities.com/fairbank56/`): Links to topographic map sources and tools.

LostOutdoors (`www.lostoutdoors.com`): This site's information is limited to the United States, but Kelly Markwell (this book's technical editor), swears by it because you can specify a point, then have it superimposed on your choice of either a topographic map or a satellite image, and you have some choice in formats. When I tried it, I could not get anything to show up but the point I provided on a black background—probably some problem with the way my browser is configured. But given his recommendation, I would suggest it as a tool.

Mapquest (`www.mapquest.com/maps`): Maps by address, zip code, or city. You can get a map with lat/lon coordinates, but you can't get it from the main interface anymore. You must go to `http://www.mapquest.com/maps/latlong.adp`, but there are rumors that the feature may eventually be removed, so use it while it's available.

Maporama (`www.maporama.com`): Maps by address around the world; you specify coordinates and in return get a map showing the spot.

MapsOnUs (`www.mapsonus.com`): You provide a street address and get a map with the coordinates of the point you specify.

MapTools (`www.maptools.com`): The site sells coordinate grids, corner rulers, and lat/lon rulers, and also has useful information on maps and grids.

MultiMap (`www.multimap.com`): Maps and aerial photography. The site claims to be available for much of the world, but the clickable zoom feature on maps seems to work best in the United Kingdom and Europe. Maps by address provide coordinates, but to within 300 feet (100 meters) accuracy. You can also provide the coordinates for a spot, and the site will display a map showing the location.

National Geographic Maps and Geography (`www.nationalgeographic.com/maps/`): Online store for maps and map software.

"Reading Topographic Maps" (`www.map-reading.com`): Free online resource for learning to read topographic maps.

"Using the UTM/MGRS Map Coordinate System" (`http://www.maptools.com/UsingUTM/index.html`): A valuable MapTools tutorial on this grid system.

Coordinates

Distance calculator (`www.wcrl.ars.usda.gov/cec/java/lat-long.htm`): Find either the surface distance (assuming straight line) or great circle distance (real travel distance over the globe) between coordinates.

Forward Inverse (`www.mentorsoftwareinc.com/PRODUCTS/FWDINV.HTM`): Free software product for either finding a second coordinate given the first, an azimuth, and a distance, or for finding the distance between two coordinates.

Getty Thesaurus of Geographic Names (`www.getty.edu/research/tools/vocabulary/tgn/`): Find the latitude and longitude for all kinds of places around the world.

Maptran (`www.ualberta.ca/~norris/navigation/maptran.html`): Translates between datums and coordinate systems.

NADCON Computations (`www.ngs.noaa.gov/cgi-bin/nadcon.prl`): Convert coordinates between NAD 27 and NAD 83 (WGS84) datums.

U.S. Gazetteer (`www.census.gov/cgi-bin/gazetteer`): Find latitude and longitude for places or zip codes in the United States.

USGS Geographic Names Information System (`geonames.usgs.gov/pls/gnis/web_query.gnis_web_query_form`): Find latitude and longitude for places in the United States.

ZIP Lookup (`www.usps.com/ncsc/lookups/lookup_ctystzip.html`): Find zip codes associated with cities in the United States.

GPS

FAA Satellite Navigation (`http://gps.faa.gov`): Information on GPS and the Federal Aviation Administration's enhancement, WAAS.

GPS Standard Positioning Service Performance Standards (`www.navcen.uscg.gov/gps/geninfo/2001SPSPerformanceStandardFINAL.pdf`): A technical publication of the U.S. Department of Defense telling you more than you ever wanted to know about GPS.

GPS Utility (`www.gpsu.co.uk`): Program for manipulating GPS information.

GPSInformation.Net (`www.gpsinformation.net`):Joe Mehaffey, Jack Yeazel, and Dale DePriest's GPS information Web site is good for GPS information and receiver reviews.

OziExplorer (**www.oziexplorer.com**): Shareware GPS mapping software that will work with most of the major brand receivers.

Topografix (**www.topografix.com**): GPS software vendor. Offers the free EasyGPS, as well as the fuller features of ExpertGPS and PanTerra.

U.S. Coast Guard Navigation Center (**www.navcen.uscg.gov/gps**): Extensive information about GPS.

USDA Forest Service GPS Home Page (**www.fs.fed.us/database/ gps/welcome.htm**): Links to GPS information and receiver performance reports.

Meeting the Outdoors

Equipment

Backpacker.com (**www.backpacker.com**): Web site of *Backpacker* magazine. Stop by for the gear reviews and articles.

Brazos Oaks (**www.brazossticks.com/index.html**): Walking sticks.

Climbing Online (**www.climbing.com**): *Climbing* magazine's site. Should you develop the taste for this version of extreme geocaching, this might be a good stop.

Eastern Mountain Sports (**www.ems.com**): Outdoor gear and clothing. Look for seasonal sales and store brands that can keep prices down. Very good with taking returns if you aren't happy with a product.

Forestry Suppliers Inc. (**www.forestry-suppliers.com**): A place to find professional and unusual equipment for the outdoors.

Kayak Online (**www.kayakonline.com**): Kayaks to the right of you, kayaks to the left of you, a kayak beneath you. Here is information on instruction and books, choosing a kayak, and even where to buy a new or used kayak.

Offroute.com (**www.offroute.com**): GPS receivers, weather instruments, other gadgets, and books and maps for the outdoors enthusiast.

Outside Online (**www.outsideonline.com**): Another major outdoors magazine.

Paddling.net (**www.paddling.net**): When it comes to canoeing or kayaking, this site can guide you to reviews, articles, and instruction.

REI (www.rei.com): Along with EMS, one of the two major online and chain store sources for outdoor gear and clothing. Also has sales. One difference is that REI is a coop; purchase a membership for a one-time fee of $15, and as long as you buy something every year, you get an annual rebate on most purchases of up to 10 percent.

Scuba Diving (www.scubadiving.com): Web site for Rodale's magazine *Scuba Diving*. Having obtained my own certification, I can heartily recommend the activity. This is a spot for reviews based on some reasonably rigorous testing as well as great information on technique.

Hiking and Backpacking

Canada Trails (www.canadatrails.ca): Extensive trail guides to Canada, whether backpacking, biking, or skiing.

Hiking & Backpacking: A Trailside Guide by Karen Berger (W.W. Norton & Co., Inc., 1995): Karen is a colleague and fellow member of the American Society of Journalists and Authors, but I actually first came across this book in a store. It's intelligent and clear, well-designed, and the author, as I learned, has successfully hiked the three long trails in the United States: the Appalachian, the Pacific Crest, and the Continental Divide. I bow to the boots of experience.

Leave No Trace (www.lnt.org): Leave No Trace is a nonprofit that promotes respect for the wilderness and outdoor ethics.

The Complete Walker IV by Colin Fletcher and C. L. Rawlins (Alfred A. Knopf, 2002): It is difficult for me to describe my delight in various versions of this book over the last 20-odd years that I've been a reader. Fletcher took on Rawlins in this latest version, and not only does the information remain keen and weighty, but the writing is an absolute delight. Kudos to the editor who brought together two separate voices into such a seamless and elegant example of human expression.

The Trail Database (www.traildatabase.org): A massive collection of links to hiking trail listings around the world. It's sites like these that make you wonder how anyone can maintain such a project without asking for money.

TheBackpacker.com (www.thebackpacker.com): Information on trails around the United States.

Canoeing and Kayaking

Kayak Essentials by Bob Beazley (Menasha Ridge Press, 1994): Learn about proper strokes, gear, river safety, and more.

Kayaking Made Easy: A Manual for Beginners with Tips for the Experienced by Dennis Stuhaug (Globe Pequot Press, 1998): Some people find it too simplistic and think the humor is lacking, but this is an undeniably popular written introduction to the activity.

The Complete Book of Canoeing: The Only Canoeing Book You'll Ever Need by I. Herbert Gordon (Globe Pequot Press, 2001): A book aimed at the beginner, but with some information the intermediate paddler will appreciate.

Climbing

Mountaineering: The Freedom of the Hills by The Mountaineers Club, Don Graydon, and Kurt Hanson (The Mountaineers Books, 1997): Fifth edition of what had become the leading guide to climbing, whether rock, ice, snow, or alpine.

Rockclimbing.com (**www.rockclimbing.com**): An online rock climbing community, with guides to climbing routes around the world and informative articles written by people who climb because it's there.

UK Climbing (**www.ukclimbing.net**): Actually a general guide to climbing, no matter where you are. The information seems a windfall for the novice.

First Aid

American Red Cross Courses (**www.redcross.org/services/hss/courses/**): One of the primary sources for first aid training. Just make sure that you take a course that does not assume the availability of a nearby hospital.

American Safety & Health Institute (**www.ashinstitute.com**): Among other things, this organization offers wilderness first aid courses and also has a book on the subject.

Backcounty First Aid and Extended Care by Buck Tilton (Globe Pequot Press, 2002): A pocket-sized guide to first aid in the woods.

Michael Hodgson's Adventure Network (www.adventurenetwork.com): Look at the *First Aid & Safety* link for some significant advice on first aid.

NOLS Wilderness First Aid by Tod Schimelpfenig and Linda Lindsey (Stackpole Books, 2000): A wilderness first aid reference book based on National Outdoor Leadership Schools training.

Wilderness Emergency Care (www.wildernessemergencycare.com): Site of Steve Donelan, an outdoor first aid expert and trainer.

Wilderness First Aid: A Pocket Guide (McGraw-Hill, 2001): A portable guide written by a board-certified specialist in emergency medicine.

Weather

The Avalanche Center (www.csac.org): Worldwide avalanche conditions and information.

BBC Weather World (www.bbc.co.uk/weather/world/): Weather information and forecasts for more than 5,000 locations around the world.

The Weather Channel (www.weather.com): U.S. weather forecasts by city or zip code.

Scuba Diving

NAUI Online (www.naui.org): A leading organization for dive training and certification. The site has links to affiliated shops for instruction.

NOAA Diving Manual: Diving for Science and Technology, edited by James Joiner (Best Publishing Company, 2001): A highly regarded general manual on scuba.

PADI (www.padi.com): The Professional Association of Dive Instructors (PADI) is the dive instruction organization with the largest number of affiliated instructors, shops, and resorts. The Web site can direct you to nearby sources of instruction around the world for dive certification.

U.S. Navy Diving Manual: A premier work on diving by people who make it their business to know. If you have a broadband connection, you can download it by going to the U.S. Navy's SEA DOC site (www.supsalv.org) and checking the links for diving publications. There are also links for ordering the book, though it can be pricy.

Geocaching

Cache Web Sites

Buxley's Geocaching Waypoint (`http://www.brillig.com/geocaching/`): This is the prime site for finding where caches lie on a map.

Geocaching.com (`www.geocaching.com`): Largest site for caches.

Navicache (`www.navicache.com`): Much smaller than Geocaching.com, but still worth checking out.

Opencaching.com (`www.geocachingworldwide.com`): Not a list of caches, but an independent discussion forum for the activity.

General Information

Clayjar's Geocache Rating System (`www.clayjar.com/gcrs/`): Get suggestions for rating the terrain and difficulty of your cache.

Geocaching Meetup (`http://geo.meetup.com`): An online system arranging meetings of geocachers. Unfortunately, few people at the time of writing had signed up, so your local meeting might be sparse.

Geocaching with Kids (`www.eduscapes.com/geocaching/kids.htm`): Some sensible ideas of how to improve the geocaching experience of your kids.

Ideology Geocaching (`http://ideology.geocaching.com.au`): Extreme Australian geocaching. Either take part or get some ideas for your neck of the woods, mate.

Markwell's FAQ Update (`http://www.markwell.us/`): Great list of questions, answers, information, and resources from the technical editor of this book. Scroll down and look for *My Personal Updates to the Geocaching FAQ*, and don't neglect the other interesting information he has amassed.

Related Activities

Geodashing (`http://geodashing.gpsgames.org`): Play on teams to visit waypoints near you.

Geodashing Golf (`http://golf.gpsgames.org`): Players go to 18 randomly chosen spots with GPS receivers.

MinuteWar (www.minutewar.org): Capture the flag using the globe as your playground.

The Degree Confluence Project (www.confluence.org): Help document every intersection of whole number latitude and longitude.

Utah Cache Games (www.cachunuts.com): Example of how one site expands on the idea of geocaching for a specific area (Utah).

Regional Web Sites

Arizona Geocaching: www.azgeocaching.com

Central Oklahoma area: http://okgeocaching.com

Central Oregon Geocaching (COGEO): www.cogeo.org

Chicago Geocaching: www.chicagogeocaching.com

GeocacheUK.com: www.geocacheuk.com

Geocachers of Central Kentucky (GEOCKY): www.geocky.org

Georgia Geocachers Association: www.ggaonline.org

Great Plains Geocaching: www.gpgeocaching.com

Idaho Geocachers: http://idahogeocachers.org

Louisiana Geocaching: http://www.lageocaching.com/

Michigan Geocaching Organization (MiGO): www.mi-geocaching.org

Middle Tennessee Geocachers Club: http://pub64.ezboard.com/bmiddletennesseegeocachers

Missoula Organization Of Geocachers [MOOG]: www.smartgroups.com/groups/moog/

New England Geocaching: http://ne.geocaching.com

Northern Nevada Geocachers: groups.yahoo.com/group/GBESGeocachers

Ozark Mountain Geocachers: www.groups.yahoo.com/group/ozmtngeocachers/

St. Louis Area Geocachers Association (SLAGA): www.geostl.com

Southeast Texas Geocachers: www.houstoncachers.org

Springfield, Missouri Geocachers: www.groups.yahoo.com/group/
Springfield_Geocachers/

Tallahassee Area Geocachers (TAG): www.nettally.com/gohlke/
geocaching/

Texas Geocaching Association: http://www.texasgeocaching.com/

Tulsa Area Geocachers: http://www.members.cox.net/geocache

Utah Association of Geocachers (UTAG): http://www.utahgeocachers.com/

Washington State Geocaching Association: www.geocachingwa.org

Wisconsin Geocaching Association (WGA): http://www.wi-geocaching.com

Cache Containers and Army Surplus

Bananas, Inc. (www.bananasinc.com/main.html): Army Navy surplus

CheaperThanDirt.com (www.cheaperthandirt.com): Military surplus, ammo
cans, camping needs, and electronics.

Tracking Objects

Books

BookCrossing (www.bookcrossing.com): Register books and follow their
progress.

Money

EuroBillTracker (www.eurobilltracker.com): For euros, the currency used
by many European nations.

DoshTracker (www.doshtracker.co.uk): Track U.K. currency.

The Note (www.sedlen.dk): Danish tracking of Danish currency (the krone).

Where's George? (www.wheresgeorge.com): For U.S. currency.

Where's The Money (www.wheresthemoney.nl): Dutch site for tracking euros.

Where's Willy? (www.whereswilly.com): Canadian currency.

Wo ist Mein Geld? (www.woistmeingeld.de): Meaning *Where is my money?* in German, it tracks euros auf Deutsch.

Outdoor Safety

Being on a mountain or in the woods is wonderful if you want to get away from it all, but it may not seem so wonderful if someone in your party has medical problems and needs help.

Certainly it's advisable to have someone with some first aid training and experience in any group going out beyond the bounds of suburbia. However, the training needs to be the right type. According to outdoor first aid expert Steve Donelan, although typical first aid courses are fine in the realm of civilization as we know it, they depend on the availability of medicines, professional backup, and even the occasional ambulance. When you are out seriously geocaching, any of these resources could well be unavailable. The difficulty people face in such a situation is the need to improvise and make do with what is at hand. Specialized training specific to wilderness or outdoors first aid is most useful. Appendix A suggests some potential sources of information and training, including Donelan's own site.

But aside from taking a local course (fitting in a geocache hunt during lunch break, of course), you can still learn about how to eliminate the largest potential sources of trouble:

- Heat

- Cold

- Wet

- Altitude

- Biological hazards (bugs and plants)

Although serious trouble requires serious measures, anyone can take simple steps to avoid problems and remain on the cache trail.

Heat

Heat does much more than cause perspiration stains on clothing. The human body is meant to work in a narrow range of internal temperature. Drive the heat too high, either because of the weather or a fever, and the results can range from unpleasant to deadly. If body temperature increases just five to six degrees Fahrenheit, or just a few in Celsius, cell membranes start to break down while the brain begins to cook. Doesn't sound too tasty, does it? Heat-induced problems progress through three stages:

- Heat cramps: Muscles, typically the ones doing the work (like legs while hiking) begin cramping. The source is usually a depletion of sodium and potassium.

- Heat exhaustion: A combination of dehydration and body heat, those who have it feel that they are running out of energy. They will be pale and sweaty, perhaps nauseated, possibly becoming confused or irritable, and sometimes experiencing loss of balance. The circulatory system must continue to deliver oxygen and nutrients and deliver heat to the skin, but dehydration causes the body to fight this by bringing the blood to the vital organs. And so the heat builds up, increasing dehydration and problems.

- Heat stroke: The most serious condition, heat stroke is a dangerous combination of body heat and dehydration. According to Donelan, the textbook symptoms are red, hot, and dry skin; these symptoms come from dehydration, but enough heightened activity in the wilderness can drive a body into the danger zone without those telltale signs. When you are away from civilization, the more reliable indicator is irrational behavior that can escalate to belligerence and a lack of cooperation.

The causes are the same—progressive degrees of excess heat compounded by dehydration. The danger is that vigorous exercise can increase a body's heat production by six to ten times, which will have the same effect has hot weather or a fever. The body doesn't care about the heat source; it still must regulate its temperature. Many years ago, I was running in a road race (back when I was svelte enough to trot with impunity). The temperature was in the 80s, and I was drinking water at the aid stations. Still, by the time I returned from the six miles, I could not walk in a straight line. It was classic heat exhaustion.

You don't have to be running to hit a problem. Although hiking seems less strenuous, you can still encounter problems, depending on conditions. Carrying a pack increases exertion and the accompanying heat production, as does moving over rougher terrain. Trying to beat everyone else for a first find of a cache can cause you to move faster and, again, drive up the internal temperature. If you are unaccustomed to being out and about on trails, enthusiasm might trick you into exerting yourself more than usual without taking proper precautions.

Even activities seemingly immune to temperature increases can cause heat problems. For example, I can remember becoming nauseous from the heat while scuba diving. One might think that immersion in water would have a naturally cooling effect; in fact, divers must avoid too much body heat loss caused by cool water. But the diver still must get into the ocean. In my case, I was diving locally in New England—not known for its tepid coastal waters— which were running in the 60s. Even in August, divers need a full wet suit. On this particular day, though, the air temperature was in the 90s, and diving, although seemingly easy, requires much more energy than the uninitiated might think, particularly if you have to walk a quarter mile in a wet suit while carrying all your gear—all told, well over 50 pounds. The result was excessive body heat.

The weather also has its effects, both obvious and subtle. Everyone knows to be careful of summer's heat. But even in winter it is possible to become over-heated if you wear too many layers of clothing. When I hike on a fairly cold New England day, I'll often wear a long-sleeved, thin hiking shirt or long underwear top and a windproof shell for my torso, and windproof winter hiking trousers. Any more, and I get too hot. Humidity is an additional complication, because it can prevent sweat from evaporating off the skin.

One way to judge the potential for trouble is to take the sum of the out-door temperature (in Fahrenheit) and the relative humidity. If the sum is higher than 160, danger is elevated and you should avoid exertion. An example of conditions that exceed the 160 level is 95 degrees with 70 percent humidity (sum of 165). In those conditions, even a good cache seems less interesting than a tropical drink and large fan. According to some experts, if the sum tops 180, just stay out of the heat.

The easiest way to cope with heat problems is to avoid them in the first place. Dress appropriately, including a hat to keep the sun from baking your head. A scarf tucked under the hat so it hangs down and protects the back of your neck can be a good addition. For both greater protection and even com-fort, you can soak the hat and scarf with water, creating a portable air-condi-tioner.

Keep drinking and eating. The proper food provides a steady supply of potassium and sodium, electrolytes necessary for your body's proper operation. Lightly salted trail mix, a combination of dried fruit and nuts, is an excellent choice. The salt provides sodium, and the fruit and nuts are good sources of potassium. Fresh fruit also has potassium, but not in such concentrated form.

Let the liquid be water; avoid sugary drinks, because they actually tax your digestive system. Unfortunately, beer, which I once thought was high in elec-trolytes, isn't, which means I will need another excuse. What doesn't change, though, is the volume that you must drink: prodigious amounts. By the time you are sweating heavily and thirsty, your body has a fluid deficit; once behind, it's difficult to catch up, because the digestive system can absorb only about a quart or liter of water an hour. It is possible to drink too much, but that is rare and would involve imbibing more water than you are likely to be able to rea-sonably carry. To keep pace, it's best to plan regular eating and drinking. On a longer hike, you can do that when you take your hourly break for five or ten minutes. But most cache hunts require relatively short hikes of under an hour, so sipping a bit while on the move should be fine.

Dehydration can progress quickly to heat exhaustion or even stroke, depending on your activity level. At the first signs of trouble, take preventative measures before conditions become worse. Get the person (or yourself) out of the sun, rest, and start fluids. Introducing electrolytes at this point is important, but food is no longer the way to do so. Digestion requires additional water and can increase dehydration. You can use a commercial electrolyte replacement formula, but cut it by half with additional water; the sugar in most such drinks will slow the rate at which the body absorbs water. You can make your own by mixing a half teaspoon of salt, a half teaspoon of baking soda, and a quarter teaspoon of salt substitute (potassium chloride) for each quart or liter of water. Wrap individual doses in wax paper and put them in an empty film canister.

If, heaven forbid, someone in your party develops heat exhaustion or stroke, it will be up to the others to recognize it and take swift action, because the victim is unlikely to be clear-headed enough to recognize the problem. In the case of heat exhaustion, get the person out of the sun, start rehydrating, and fan to gently cool. For heat stoke, time is of the essence. Cool the person by whatever means available. Supporting someone in a stream, lake, or ocean is good. If there is no body of water, get your comrade into the shade and cool aggressively by putting wet cloths on the body (especially the head) and fanning.

Heat cramps require action too, but they are not a life-and-death matter. Stretch the muscles and gently massage them while providing liquid with electrolytes.

Cold

Just as too much heat is a problem, so is too little. The human body does poorly outside of a narrow band of internal temperatures. In short, when it's cold outside, dress warmly like mother always said, using layers and non-cotton materials, as Chapter 5 suggests. Be sure to cover that head, which vents 40 to 70 percent of the heat from your body, depending on whether there is a wind.

Someone inadequately protected from the cold will be the last person to know it. First, judgment and reason go, followed by coordination, movement, and speech. If you are out in real cold, it is vital that you and your companions keep an eye and ear on each other. Should someone have trouble, be sure to replace wet clothing with dry, get a hat on a bare head, and then get that person into a sleeping bag or, if you don't have one, the emergency space blanket that should be in your caching pack. To increase the warming effect, if there is room, bundle in a second person to act like a human furnace.

In the preventative vein, continuous munching is a good idea in the cold, because the process keeps a steady source of fuel that the body can use to produce heat. Carbohydrates are best, because metabolizing fat requires more water and oxygen. Also, keep drinking; although it may sound odd, dehydration is just as big a problem in the cold as it is in the heat. But because the air is usually dry, sweat often evaporates without making its presence known, unlike on a hot day. You also lose moisture when exhaling.

People often think of frostbite as the chief danger from the cold, but according to Donelan, "South of the Arctic circle, you almost have to do something stupid to get frost bite." However, it can still happen, especially on a cold day when the wind also picks up, so wear gloves. (I prefer mittens with glove liners and a zippered side, so I can get my fingers out when I need dexterity.) Avoid tightly lacing your boots, which can reduce circulation and its accompanying flow of heat, and in very cold weather, consider trading the gaiters in for *super gaiters*, a type with pockets for insulating foam. Boots should be well waterproofed.

Altitude

At sea level, there is "one atmosphere" of pressure, because all of Earth's atmosphere is sitting on our heads. As we move higher, like up a mountain, less air is overhead, so less pressure bears down on us. As the pressure drops, so does the number of oxygen molecules in a given volume of air. So, when you breath at altitude, your body must work harder to get the oxygen it needs.

You would think that the body would try to take in more oxygen, and you would be correct. But the way the body does that is through chemistry. Breathing is triggered by increased levels of acid in the blood. As carbon dioxide—an acid—builds up in your blood, your body breathes. But when the oxygen drops, so does the amount of carbon dioxide your body manufactures, because oxygen is one of the substances required to make carbon dioxide; and so, your breathing doesn't increase, and you don't get more oxygen, leaving you fatigued. That intelligent body does notice a problem, so it increases the amount of acid in the bloodstream, which makes you breath more, thereby bringing more oxygen into your system.

Given time, your body does its job and acclimates itself to altitude. And that is the trick—give yourself enough time. When going after a cache at a higher altitude, take a day or two before you start strenuous activity. If you go high enough, above 7,000 or 8,000 feet, it's possible to develop acute mountain sickness, or AMS. The symptoms can include headache, nausea, a lack of energy, and sleeping trouble. In such a case, stop climbing and drink fluids. Should things not improve, descend 1,000 or 2,000 feet and let your body acclimate. In rare cases, you could develop high-altitude cerebral edema, or fluid on the brain, which seriously affects thinking and motor skills; you'd be incapable of passing the sobriety test of walking heel-to-toe along a straight line. The solution is to immediately descend to lower altitudes and seek medical aid. The other highly unusual problem is high altitude pulmonary edema, or fluid in the lungs. Its symptoms include failure to acclimate, continued heavy breathing, and an inability to recover energy after resting. Two other symptoms are a resting pulse higher than 100 and a crackling sound in the lungs when breathing (you can hear this by putting your ear to the affected person's ribcage). Again, the solution is to immediately descend to lower elevations, and then seek medical aid.

Biological Hazards

From rattlesnakes and scorpions to poison ivy, oak, and sumac, many things in nature can make you regret not having a biohazard suit. Forewarned is forearmed, however, and by taking care and notice of your surroundings, you can happily go looking for cache after cache without developing rash after rash.

First step is to get a book on hiking in whatever area you plan to travel. Find out about the denizens of the area and any potential problems. Remember that you are a guest in the outdoors, and behave accordingly. Don't blindly thrust your hands, nose, or any other appendage behind a rock, under a log, or into a cave. If probe you must, gently use your walking stick which, after all, is expendable. Watch your step to avoid disturbing some member of nature's family.

In geocaching, aside from looking into spots that might be either caches or habitats, irritating plants can be a hazard. Learn to recognize the three major offenders—poison oak, poison sumac, and poison ivy—on sight.

Look for these plants' characteristics. Poison ivy grows with clusters of three pointed leaves, the middle longer than the other two. The leaves' edges can be toothed or smooth, so don't assume that you are safe because they are one way when you think they must be the other. The leaves are reddish in spring, turn to green through summer, and take on autumnal colors in the fall. You might also see bunches of small greenish flowers near the junction of the leaves and the stem. Plants can be vines, a trailing shrub, or a free-standing shrub.

Many people may know the "leaves of three, let it be" rhyme, but that does no good if you are looking at poison sumac or at non-conformist poison oak. Poison sumac grows in boggy areas and is a tall—up to 15 feet—shrub with three to six pairs of smooth-edged leaflets and one at the end of each branch. Depending on the time of year, it may have clusters of pale yellow or cream-colored berries. Poison oak can be a low shrub, a clump up to six feet tall, or vines up to thirty feet long. The leaves look like oak leaves, generally in clusters of three, and can have clusters of yellow berries.

Not everyone is bothered, but a good 85 percent of the populace will develop an allergic reaction, so don't take chances. If you think you've been exposed, you have about ten minutes at most before the urushiol, the active ingredient, begins to penetrate the skin. Kelly Markwell keeps a container of antihistamine spray for such occasions to put off any immediate allergic reactions. But the thing to do as quickly as possible, according to the U.S. Food and Drug Administration, is to first clean the area if possible with rubbing alcohol, then wash with water. Now you've removed enough of the excess urushiol to change to soap and water without the danger of spreading the chemical even farther. This may not let you avoid the rash, but it will at least reduce the severity. Also, while wearing gloves, wipe off exposed clothing and boots with alcohol and water.

If moving through nonpoisonous grass and brush in a tick-prone area, have everyone in your party wear long trousers, possibly pulling socks over the cuffs to eliminate that opening, and check for ticks after you return to the car. Lyme disease is an unnecessary risk. Then there is the entire retinue of other insects ready to bug you: mosquitoes, no-see-ums, greenhead and blackhead flies, and other hungry flying extroverts. They are generally out in summer, so bring insect repellent.

Finally, remember that preparation and care should not keep you from enjoying the outdoors. On the contrary, it will improve your experience, and keep you from regretting it.

Index

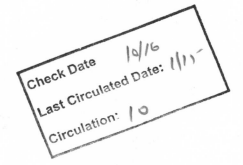
Printed in the United States
147825LV00003BA/66/A

9 781590 591222